PLANETARY GODS
AND PLANETARY ORDERS
IN THE MYSTERIES OF MITHRAS

ÉTUDES PRÉLIMINAIRES
AUX RELIGIONS ORIENTALES
DANS L'EMPIRE ROMAIN

PUBLIÉES PAR

M. J. VERMASEREN†

M. E. C. VERMASEREN-VAN HAAREN et **MARGREET B. DE BOER**

TOME CENT-NEUVIÈME

ROGER BECK

PLANETARY GODS
AND PLANETARY ORDERS
IN THE MYSTERIES OF MITHRAS

ROGER BECK

PLANETARY GODS
AND PLANETARY ORDERS
IN THE MYSTERIES OF MITHRAS

WITH A FRONTISPIECE, 5 FIGURES AND 6 PLATES

E. J. BRILL
LEIDEN • NEW YORK • KØBENHAVN • KÖLN
1988

This book has been published with the help of a grant from the Canadian Federation for the Humanities, using funds provided by the Social Sciences and Humanities Research Council of Canada.

Library of Congress Cataloging-in-Publication Data

Beck, Roger.
  Planetary gods and planetary orders in the mysteries
of Mithras.

  (Etudes préliminaires aux religions orientales dans
l'Empire romain ; t. 109)
  Bibliography: p.
  Includes index.
  1. Mithraism.   2. Planets—Religious aspects.
I. Title.   II. Series.
BL1585.B43   1987   299'.15   87-30906
ISBN 90-04-08450-9

ISSN 0531-1950
ISBN 90 04 08450 9

PRINTED IN THE NETHERLANDS BY E. J. BRILL

εἰ δὲ καὶ τῆς ἀρρήτου μυσταγωγίας ἀφαίμην
ἣν ὁ Χαλδαῖος περὶ τὸν ἑπτάκτινα θεὸν ἐβάκχευσεν
ἀνάγων δί αὐτοῦ τὰς ψυχάς
ἄγνωστα ἐρῶ

To my wife, Janet

CONTENTS

Plates I-IV

PREFACE

This study opens with a "mystery" — in the modern sense of the word: why did Mithraism, in assigning the seven planets as tutelary powers to its hierarchy of grades of initiation, set them in a novel and unique order; what was the logic of that order's construction, and to what meanings did it give expression? That initial puzzle, however, proves in the answering to be but a part of a larger, very much more complex and more fundamental question of the role of *several* planetary orders in the doctrines, viz. the soteriology and theology, of the cult. For the grade order was not the only order in which the Mysteries deployed the planets, and an enquiry into the significance of those orders in context necessitates an exploration of a number of far from simple monuments, not to mention the difficult literary text on Mithraic planetary ordering, Origen *Contra Celsum* 6.22. As so often in Mithraic studies, the enquiry takes the path of cumulative reflections on, and analyses of, certain of the great (though not necessarily in size), complex and problematic icons of the bull-killing, the tauroctonies so-called: in the present study, the relief from Bologna (*CIMRM* 693), the "monument of Ottaviano Zeno" (335), and the fresco of the Barberini Mithraeum (390). The last two may come as a surprise, for the planets are there represented only by a row of altars. Much, however, is discoverable therefrom. And introduced there, and implicated, as I argue, in the whole process of the initiate's passage of the planets, is that strange being of the Mysteries, the lion-headed, snake-encircled deity. The study offers a number of conclusions on that figure, remote though he might seem from its proper subject.

The reader will find here a number of new propositions on the doctrines of the cult, its theology and soteriology. Two principles, especially, inform the study, and these it has been my main purpose to demonstrate and to seek to establish: first, that Mithraism was a learned religion that drew on, and adapted to its doctrines, elements of contemporary learning — in the present case, the "science" of astrology. In so doing, it legitimized itself as a teaching which reflected the "real" world as learned men supposed it to be. Yet by adapting and distorting that learning into new patterns and new uses, it could also claim the special esoteric "truths" so essential to such a cult. Secondly, the concern with the planets and their ordering was no mere intellectual game. The planets, and in particular the sequences into which they could be set, mattered to the cult because they were implicated in a complex fashion in the great celestial journey, the ascent of the soul which was the principal business of the Mysteries. This is not a fashionable view of the Mysteries, any more than is the conception of them as a learned religion (although R. Merkelbach's recent

Mithras [below, n. 4] may somewhat redress the balance on both scores); but I am convinced, and the present study aims throughout to demonstrate, that it is the correct one. As the Emperor Julian said in another context and of another mystery (175B): αὐτῆς δὲ τῆς ἁγνείας φαμὲν τὸν σκοπὸν ἄνοδον τῶν ψυχῶν.

That the Mysteries were thoroughly impregnated with astrological lore is one of my fundamental postulates. Although the presence of learned astrology is demonstrated again and again in the course of the study, it would be as well to be explicit about it here at the outset. It is not merely that the monuments are awash with astrological symbols — Sun, Moon, stars, planets, and signs of the zodiac. More significantly, of the few extant literary references to the cult a remarkably high proportion relate to astrological matters. This fact was acknowledged by the first and greatest of modern Mithraic scholars, Franz Cumont: "Ces explications [i.e. the astrological ones] ... sont celles que les auteurs anciens ont le plus souvent transmises" (*TMMM* 1.198). Cumont supposed, however, that this was merely because these doctrines were secondary and marginal and could therefore be divulged with impunity: "les propos d'antichambre dont on entretenait les prosélytes de la porte avant de les admettre à la connaissance de la doctrine ésotérique et de leur révéler les traditions iraniennes sur l'origine et la fin de l'homme et du monde" (*ibid.* 202). A simpler hypothesis — and one which predicates no vanished oriental corpus — is that the astrological doctrines preponderate precisely because they were of central importance, not of course as the sole matter of the Mysteries nor the sole metaphor or vehicle of their teaching, but at the heart nonetheless. Why they mattered has been suggested already: they furnished the framework for the Mysteries' theories on the destiny of the soul, or at least the only framework which is still in some measure extant or recoverable by today's researcher.

Accepting astrology's centrality to the Mysteries is far from easy. As a science or an art astrology has long ago and rightly fallen into disrepute, and much of its material seems to the modern sensibility unappealing, arid or silly. Instinctively, then, one feels that such sorry and rebarbative stuff could never have lodged at the core of a real religion or have commanded the respect and attention of truly religious folk. There must, one feels, have been "something else" — Cumont's "esoteric doctrine" and "Iranian traditions," or whatever — or how is one to account for the undoubted piety of the Mysteries' devotees? Two further sorts of predisposition alienate the modern scholar from the astrological component of the Mysteries, one quite creditable, the other less so. First, it must be admitted that the astrological interpretations of ancient religions have all too often been shallow, sensationalist, and quite unconvincing. They have a dubious reputation, and the scholar is properly sceptical. Mithraism, unfortunately, has not been free of that type of interpretation, centring in recent years on somewhat facile attempts at deciphering the astrological "meaning" of the tauroctony or, worse, the celestial "identity" of the tauroctonous Mithras. Secondly, astrology is and was a technical system, and it takes a modicum of effort to learn its principles and rudiments, especially these days when we are not as routinely familiar as were our ancient predecessors with the working of the heavens and the apparent motions of the celestial bodies which constitute astrology's factual basis. It is thus a wearisome business to acquire a minimal comprehension of the system, especially when there is the prejudice that in any case it is all rather marginal to the real "religious" matter of the Mysteries. To all of which I can only reply, first, that if astrology is demonstrably present in large measure in the monuments and written evidence, then it is to astrological interpretations that we must address ourselves, in spite of disinclination or distaste; secondly, that the superficiality of previous astrological interpretations is no reason not to attempt something more profound down the same path; and, thirdly, that only on *a priori* grounds — and poor ones at that — can the astrological data and the inferences drawn therefrom be dismissed as marginal or illusory. Not a scrap of evidence suggests that the Mysteries were not fundamentally serious about their astrology, or that for the ancients, unlike us, astrology was not the true stuff of religion. Quite the contrary: there is every indication that astrology, broadly construed as a mode of knowing the universe and its work-ings, was profoundly implicated in religious thought in general, and in the Mysteries of Mithras in particular.

Inevitably, certain of the interpretations set out here are tentative, hypothetical, even speculative; for what is being interpreted is primarily the monuments, and the monuments, in default of the written teachings of the Mysteries, are mute and enigmatic, "a book without words." Certainty and final proof are therefore unattainable. That, however, does not render the making of hypotheses illegitimate — or disastrous if they are not in fact cor-rect in every detail. Ultimately, one is more concerned with capturing the quality and tenor of Mithraic doctrine (... if not precisely thus, then *like* this ...) than with fixing definitive meanings on all the minutiae. What does mat-ter, however, is that the hypotheses should be well-grounded and reasonable, that they should be rooted in the data and developed on sound and explicit calculations of their likelihood. The enemy of productive enquiry here is not speculation itself but *uncontrolled* speculation.

Fortunately, in this line of enquiry astrology itself furnishes a measure of control. Astrology is a well-defined and complex system. Its employment on the monuments leaves an unmistakable signature which is manifested pri-marily in the composition, i.e. in the arrangement of the symbols. Since it is a *known* system (a book *with* words), its presence thus reveals certain definite meanings and prompts certain rather specific questions. Two examples from the present study will illustrate the method — and show too that the only alter-

native to an astrological interpretation is to admit in case after case freak coin-
cidences which cumulatively become altogether implausible. (1) (pp. 34 ff.)
The Housesteads birth scene (*CIMRM* 860) preserves a most unusual arrangement of the zodiac; that arrangement fits the technical astrological system of
planetary "houses." The system of houses is demonstrably used on other
Mithraic monuments and arguably underlies Mithraic doctrine preserved in
one of the literary sources (Porphyry's *De antro nympharum*). Either, then,
the Housesteads monument "just happens" to fall into the pattern of
planetary houses within the Mysteries? (2) (pp. 91 ff.) It is a fact that the beam
of light linking Mithras to Sol, which is a standard feature of the composition
ceded, then it becomes not merely admissible but imperative to ask why: i.e.,
what doctrinal point underlies the use of a technical system such as the
planetary houses within the Mysteries? (2) (pp. 91 ff.) It is a fact that the beam
of light linking Mithas to Sol, which is a standard feature of the composition
of the tauroctony, in the Barberini fresco (*CIMRM* 390) passes through the
symbol of Capricorn. Capricorn, in certain astrological doctrines arguably
shared by the Mithraists, is the gate of celestial ascent for souls. Again, coincidence or design? If design, then surely it is a reasonable hypothesis that the
light beam, at least in the Barberini Mithraeum, alludes *inter alia* to the ascent
of souls.

Let these two examples suffice to illustrate what I consider the proper pur-
suit of astrological interpretations of Mithraic doctrine to explain astrological
data on Mithraic monuments. The reader will decide for him- or herself to
what extent these and other interpretations stay within the bounds of
plausibility and good sense. I am not overly troubled at pushing speculation to
the limits; for it is dull and profitless scholarship that dares not move from the
known to the unknown. Given my methods, however, I do believe that what I
propose is by and large well anchored in what the Mysteries actually taught.

Inevitably, relevant new studies will appear between the completion of a
manuscript and its publication. I regret that it was not possible to accommodate in my text or notes an excellent study of the lion-headed god which appeared in that interval, but I commend it wholeheartedly both for its coverage
of the data and for its insight into the meanings underlying that deity's fluid
iconography: H. M. Jackson, "The Meaning and Function of the Leontocephaline in Roman Mithraism," *Numen* 32 (1985), 17-45.

In conclusion, I wish to record my gratitude to the late Professor M. J. Vermaseren. It was with his kindly encouragement that I wrote this study, and he
was able to read and comment on its first complete draft before his untimely
death. My sense of loss that he did not live to see this volume through to print
is somewhat tempered by the knowledge that it and other future volumes of
the series *Études préliminaires* are in the good and experienced hands of Dr.

Margreet B. de Boer and Mrs. M. E. C. Vermaseren-van Haaren. Lastly, my thanks to Mrs. Stefanie Kennell for the compilation of the index and to Drs. and Mrs. J. J. V. M. Derksen for the preparation of the figures.

University of Toronto
January 1986

ABBREVIATIONS

CIMRM: M. J. Vermaseren, *Corpus Inscriptionum et Monumentorum Religionis Mithriacae*, 2 vols (The Hague 1956-60).

EPRO: Études préliminaires aux religions orientales dans l'Empire romain.

JMS: *Journal of Mithraic Studies*.

Mithraic Studies: J. R. Hinnells (ed.), *Mithraic Studies*: Proceedings of the First International Congress of Mithraic Studies, 2 vols (with consecutive pagination) (Manchester 1975).

Mysteria Mithrae: U. Bianchi (ed.), *Mysteria Mithrae*: Atti del Seminario Internazionale su "La specificità storico-religiosa dei Misteri di Mithra ..." (EPRO 80, Leiden 1979).

TMMM: Franz Cumont, *Textes et monuments figurés relatifs aux mystères de Mithra*, 2 vols (Brussels, I 1899, II 1896).

I

One of the most satisfying advances in our knowledge of the "oriental" and mystery cults in the Roman Empire was the discovery, towards the middle of the present century, of the exact order of the grades of initiation in Mithraism as revealed by the mosaic in the Mithraeum of Felicissimus at Ostia and by dipinti in the Sa. Prisca Mithraeum in Rome. These discoveries told us, with a certainty that is quite rare in this field, not only the precise limitations of the Mithraic *cursus* — seven grades in a given order — but also that each grade was under the protection of one of the planetary gods:

Pater	Saturn
Heliodromus	Sun
Perses	Moon
Leo	Jupiter
Miles	Mars
Nymphus	Venus
Corax	Mercury

In the Felicissimus mosaic (*CIMRM* 299)[1] this information is presented in the form of a series of compartments running ladder-like up the length of the aisle, each compartment containing three symbols, two of the grade and one of the planetary god. The symbols of the Corax and Mercury are nearest the entrance, those of the Pater and Saturn nearest the cult-niche. Since in the sequence of initiation the Corax is the junior grade and the Pater the senior, the *cursus* at Felicissimus is viewed from its point of departure, for it is from the entrance that the symbols are seen right side up. Progress up the aisle thus imitates progress through the grades:

Grade	Felicissimus symbols			Planet
	grade symbols		planetary symbols	
	(left)	(right)		
Pater	*patera* and sceptre	Phrygian cap	*falx*	Saturn
Heliodromus	torch	rayed bonnet	whip	Sun
Perses	*falx*	plough (?) and star	crescent	Moon
Leo	fire shovel	sistrum	thunderbolt	Jupiter
Miles	pack	helmet	spear	Mars
Nymphus	(missing)	diadem	lamp	Venus
Corax	raven	cup	*caduceus*	Mercury

---

[1] The mithraeum was published by G. Becatti, *Scavi di Ostia* 2: *I mitrei* (Rome 1954), 105-112.

It is not part of our task to comment on the significance of the grade symbols or the problems which they pose. Our concern is strictly with the planets, whose symbols are in fact trite and unremarkable; it is their *sequence*, as we shall soon see, which is extraordinary.[2]

At Sa. Prisca dipinti (*CIMRM* 480)[2] specify the relationship between the grades and the planets: each grade is under the *tutela*, the protective power, of a planetary god. The dipinti appear above individual representatives of the grades in a fresco on the south wall showing a procession advancing in order of seniority towards a seated Pater. The Pater, as at Felicissimus, is closest to the cult-niche of the mithraeum; the Corax, at the end of the procession, is farthest. With the exception of the Pater's, the dipinti all follow the same formula. I cite the Lion's, by way of example: *Nama Leonibus tutela Iovis*. The throned Pater is privileged with the lengthier *Nama Patribus ab oriente ad occidentem tutela Saturni*.

A function of this linking of grades to planets, one may reasonably conjecture, is to validate the cult's grade structure and in particular the *number* of its grades. It answers the question: why seven, neither more nor less? The answer: because there are seven planets, neither more nor less. But this legitimizing function leads at once to a paradox; for the *order* in which the cult set out the planets, and hence the grades, is itself in a sense illegitimate. It occurs nowhere else in antiquity. Thus it cannot answer the question why one grade precedes another by appealing to what is current in society or accepted as scientific fact. Rather, it asserts a different and idiosyncratic "truth." It says, in effect, that the universe is other than what accepted usage and scientific opinion imagine it to be. There is an arcane reality with its special succession of planets, and it is that which validates the grades of the Mysteries and the progression of initiation through them.[3]

---

[2] But see the definitive publication in M. J. Vermaseren and C. C. Van Essen, *The Excavations in the Mithraeum of the Church of Santa Prisca in Rome* (Leiden 1965), 155-158, for the correct restoration of the dipinti. *CIMRM* follows earlier false ascriptions of the Persians to Mercury and the Ravens to the Moon.

[3] I owe the concern with modes of *validation* (how does a new and marginal cult legitimize itself?) to Richard Gordon, both to his writings, some of which will be mentioned below, and to his conversation.

Lest I seem to be guessing at the logic of the Mysteries in a dangerously speculative way, let me cite a close parallel from a literary source where the argument is explicit. In his *Hymn to King Helios*, Julian, who was arguably a Mithraist, rearranges the visible cosmos by removing the sphere of the Sun beyond that of the fixed stars (*Or.* 4.148A-B, Loeb trans.):

> Some say then, even though all men are not ready to believe it, that the sun travels in the starless heavens far above the region of the fixed stars. And on this theory he will not be stationed midmost among the planets but midway between the three worlds: that is, according to the hypothesis of the mysteries, if indeed one ought to use the word "hypothesis" and not rather say "established truths," using the word "hypothesis" for the study of the heavenly bodies. For the priests of the mysteries tells us what they have been taught by the gods or mighty daemons, whereas the astronomers make plausible hypotheses from the harmony

Is the logic of this different order, and of the different reality which it implies, recoverable? Strangely enough, although the relationships between individual planets and their respective grades are treated routinely in works on the cult,[4] the fact that the order *is* unique, let alone the problem which its uniqueness poses, has scarcely been addressed.[5] And yet an answer might well elicit something of significance concerning the views of the Mysteries both on the cosmos and on the nature of the pilgrimage through the grades. If the planetary order for the grades had been one of the usual ones, its choice by the cult would perhaps have been without significance, a bland utilization of what was ready to hand. As it is, however, their discovery of a new order argues a special purpose and a special meaning. It will be the task of this study to elucidate that purpose and meaning and in so doing to explore something of the Mysteries' ideology on the universe and its powers and on the *via salutis* of initiation through the grades.

Two lines of enquiry immediately suggest themselves: first, to search for clues in the other orderings of the planets attested in the Mysteries apart from the context of the grades; secondly, to consider whether the planetary order for the grades might be explicable as a distortion of some recognized public order or as a conflation of two such orders, in which case the logic of the rear-

---

that they observe in the visible spheres. It is proper, no doubt, to approve the astronomers as well, but where any man thinks it better to believe the priests of the mysteries, him I admire and revere, both in jest and earnest.

It may well be that among the "mysteries" Julian has in mind particularly those of Mithras. For the doctrine of the Sun above the stars, outlandish from the point of view of Greek science, is Iranian orthodoxy. Possibly it represents a detail (one of the relatively few) which the cult may have inherited from its Persian antecedents, perhaps as a variant when the Sun was considered apart from the set of the seven planets in which it is embedded in Graeco-Roman thinking. That, however, is not the point at issue here, which is rather to demonstrate how special arcane "facts" from a privileged source ("the gods or mighty daemons") are used, in the teeth of both common and scientific opinion, to validate an esoteric structure — in Julian's case the placing of the Sun in the midst of the three universes (visible, intellectual and intelligible) effected by its removal to the extreme boundary of the visible world.

[4] See, e.g., M. J. Vermaseren, *Mithras, the Secret God* (trans. T. and V. Megaw, London 1963), 138-153. There are also treatments of the grade sequence apart from its planetary parameters or where the planetary *order* is not at issue: I. Tóth, "*Mithram esse coronam suam*: Bemerkungen über den dogmatischen Hintergrund der Initiationsriten der Mithrasmysterien," *Acta Classica Universitatis Scientiarum Debreceniensis* 2 (1966), 73-79; R. Merkelbach, "Weihegrade und Seelenlehre der Mithrasmysterien," Rheinisch-Westfälische Akademie der Wissenschaften, *Vorträge* G.257 (1982); *id.*, *Mithras* (Königstein/Ts. 1984), 77-133; cf. E. D. Francis, "Mithraic Graffiti from Dura-Europos," *Mithraic Studies* 424-445, at 442. These lie outside the scope of the present enquiry, but see my critique in "Mithraism since Franz Cumont," *Aufstieg und Niedergang der römischen Welt* 2.17.4.2002-2115, at 2091-93. By far the best treatment of the grades, in my view, is R. L. Gordon, "Reality, Evocation and Boundary in the Mysteries of Mithras," *JMS* 3 (1980), 19-99.

[5] An exception is U. Bianchi, "Prolegomena: The Religio-Historical Question of the Mysteries of Mithra. C. The Initiation Structure ...," *Mysteria Mithrae* 31-47, to which study I shall return below.

rangement might provide a clue to the logic of the Mithraic order so derived. The second approach will in fact yield at least a working hypothesis, and I propose to pursue it first, postponing the lengthier and more intricate exploration of the other planetary orders used by the cult.

II

It is at least *a priori* likely that the Mysteries would have adapted common usage rather than inventing an entirely new order. Even the most innovative cult, if it is to win adherents, must offer a compromise between the novel and the familiar, between its particular vision and a wider "common knowledge," between its own authority and the authority of conventional wisdom about the way the world is. It may furnish a new road to salvation, but the landmarks and their disposition must still be recognizable in general and accepted terms.[6]

At the time when Mithraism emerged in the Empire as an organized and fairly widespread cult with its apparatus, real and doctrinal, more or less in place — that is, towards the middle of the second century A.D. — there were three planetary orders commonly in use, though for different purposes. The first of these, which is the primary one in that the other two were derived from it, is the order according to supposed distance from the earth. From the most distant planet inwards it runs:

Saturn   Jupiter   Mars   Sun   Venus   Mercury   Moon.

It is based on the planets' geocentric periods of revolution: on an assumption of more or less equal speeds, the longer a planet takes to complete its orbit the further away it must be. This principle determines the positions of Saturn, Jupiter and Mars at the far end of the scale and of the Moon at the near end. It also establishes that the remaining three planets (Sun, Venus, Mercury) lie between Mars and the Moon; but it cannot fix their positions relative to each other. Viewed from the earth, Venus and Mercury accompany the Sun on its annual journey; so their periods, on average, are the same as the Sun's — one year. The system, then, is arbitrary in respect of those three planets, and variants are in fact found with virtually every combination of the three,[7] notably the sequences which place the Sun *below* Venus and Mercury:

---

[6] See the start of Gordon's "Reality, Evocation and Boundary ..." (above, n. 4), esp. 22 f.: "New cults have to cannibalize upon a whole range of banal and customary beliefs within the society in which they exist if they are to be more than minute evanescent, usually kin-based, groups."

[7] The variants are succinctly set out in O. Neugebauer, *A History of Ancient Mathematical Astronomy* (Berlin, Heidelberg and New York 1975), 2.690-693. See also F. Boll, "Hebdomas,"

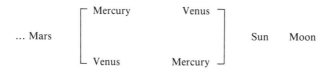

This sequence with the Sun next to the Moon, sometimes called "Egyptian" after Macrobius (*In Somn.* 1.19), derives its authority from Plato, for it is the order implied in the *Timaeus* (38D). The "Chaldean" (Macr. *ibid.*) sequence, which places the Sun in the middle in fourth place (and Mercury below Venus, as above), is generally regarded as later than the "Egyptian,"[8] even though Ptolemy (*Alm.* 9.1) ascribes it to "older" (παλαιοτέροις) authorities. The "Chaldean" order is not really a "discovery" of the sort which can be confidently attributed to a particular scientist (any more than can the "Egyptian").[9] It is better understood as a *convention* for ordering the planets according to distance which gradually won acceptance over its rival variants until in late Hellenistic astronomy it became the dominant one. Beyond the narrow circle of professional astronomers, it was adopted by Roman and Greek intellectuals, by those who for philosophical or technical purposes needed to treat of these matters; "Cicero, Vitruvius, Pliny, and Plutarch take if for granted."[10] It was basic, too, for the astrologers, who in all probability provided much of the impetus towards its acceptance.[11]

This order of the planets according to distance, in its "Chaldean" form, would be that to which, at the time of the Mysteries' formation and for well over a century before, one would naturally look to express *spatial* reality on the grand scale. The order defines the *depth* of the cosmos from its boundary at the sphere of the fixed stars to its centre, the earth. The best illustration of this is Cicero's simple and vivid description in the *Somnium Scipionis* (4), where Africanus reviews for his grandson the universe inwards from the imagined vantage point among the stars. As the same work likewise shows, the order also defines the route along which souls pass to terrestrial mortality from celestial immortality and back. The order thus carries — for those who accept such spiritual scenarios, as many then did in one form or another — a religious significance beyond the literal mapping of the heavens. In a general

---

RE 7.2.2547-78, at 2565-70; A. Bouché-Leclercq, *L'astrologie grecque* (Paris 1899 [rp. Brussels 1963]), 105-110, also 64 n. 1; J. L. E. Dreyer, *A History of Astronomy from Thales to Kepler* (Cambridge 1906 [rp. New York 1953]), 168; J. Flamant, "Sotériologie et systèmes planétaires," *La soteriologia dei culti orientali nell' Impero Romano* (edd. U. Bianchi and M. J. Vermaseren, EPRO 92, Leiden 1982), 223-242, at 228-233; P. Tannery, *Recherches sur l'histoire de l'astronomie ancienne* (Paris 1893), 126 f., 261.

[8] See preceding note.

[9] Names have been suggested, by both ancient and modern authorities, for its earliest proponents: see esp. Boll (above, n. 7), 2567.

[10] Neugebauer (above, n. 7), 691.

[11] Boll, Bouché-Leclercq (above, n. 7).

way, perfection and permanence are conceived as lying at one end of the scale, "change and decay" at the other; the sequence of the planets is the ladder between the two.[12]

In considering whether the Mithraists adapted this order, two further points are relevant. First, though called "Chaldean," the order is most certainly *not* the product of real Chaldean, i.e. Babylonian, astronomy — any more than the "Egyptian" order is truly Egyptian. Neither culture was concerned with the relative positions of the planets in spatial depth, and the attested sequences of both bear no relation to either variant of the order in question, which is purely Greek in conception.[13] In origin, as Bouché-Leclercq suggested,[14] the label "Chaldean" may have signified no more than that the order was that favoured and promoted by astrologers, the term astrologer and Chaldean being in certain contexts synonymous. Macrobius (*In Somn.* 1.19), however, obviously intends Chaldean in the sense of Babylonian, but for how long before his day the order was so understood we do not know. Thus we cannot say whether for the contemporaries of the early Mithraists it would have carried exotic and oriental connotations which might have recommended it to this avowedly "Persian" cult.

Secondly, it is universally agreed that a decisive factor in favour of the "Chaldean" order was its setting of the Sun in fourth place at the exact mid point of the sequence. With that arrangement the Sun achieves a position consonant with its dignity and pre-eminence, a position from which it may better orchestrate the dance of the stars and the rhythms of the cosmos. Again, one need only cite the *Somnium Scipionis* (4) to that effect: *mediam regionem sol obtinet, dux et princeps et moderator luminum reliquorum.*[15] From our point of view, however, this poses something of a paradox. If, as I shall suggest, the Mithraists adapted this "Chaldean" order by conflating it with another given and public order so as to produce their own private order, it appears that in effecting the rearrangement they sacrificed precisely the feature of the "Chal-

---

[12] Ideas about the descent and reascent of the soul and the sources in which they are found are examined by D. W. Bousset, "Die Himmelsreise der Seele," *Archiv für Religionswissenschaft* 4 (1901), 136-169, 229-273, and P. Capelle, *De luna, stellis, lacteo orbe animarum sedibus* (diss. Halle 1917); also in important recent articles by J. Flamant (above, n. 7), and I. P. Culianu, "L'ascension de l'âme' dans les mystères et hors des mystères," *ibid.* 276-302; finally, in a recent monograph by Culianu: *Psychanodia I: A Survey of the Evidence Concerning the Ascension of the Soul and its Relevance* (EPRO 99, Leiden 1983). That the Mithraists subscribed to a version of these views will be argued below.

[13] Neugebauer (above, n. 7), 690 f.; *id.*, *The Exact Sciences in Antiquity* (New York 1969 [rp. Providence, R.I., 1957]), 168-170. Dreyer (above, n. 7) is in error here. Either variant (or both) may of course be Egyptian in the trivial sense of having been formulated on Egyptian soil — in that great centre of Greek astronomy and astrology, Alexandria.

[14] (above, n. 7), 108 f.

[15] The numerous references to this view of the Sun as the animator of the universe at the centre of the planets are set out and examined by Franz Cumont in "la théologie solaire du paganisme romain," *Mémoires présentés ... à l'Academie des Inscriptions et Belles-Lettres* 12, Pt. 2 (1913), 447-479, at 451 f.

dean'' order which might seem the most tailored to their ideology. It is a truism that Mithraism was a solar cult and its god the Unconquered Sun. And yet in making its disposition of the planets the Mysteries placed the Sun neither at the head of the sequence nor at its centre and heart, although the latter position was sanctioned by the most popular and basic planetary order of the times and by the uranography of which that order was the expression. Taken from this perspective, perhaps the most important question to ask of the Mithraic planetary order is not why the Sun is where it is but why it is *not* elsewhere. One looks, in other words, for some overriding factor of great cogency which has drawn the Sun away from the place of honour either at the head or in the centre of the sequence.

The second planetary order current at the time need not detain us long. It belongs exclusively to the art of astrology, though as being familiar to clients as well as practitioners it will have been quite widely known. It is the order in which the planets appear almost invariably in early papyrus horoscopes (before A.D. 150) and in the literary horoscopes of all dates.[16] Unlike the order by distance, the horoscopic order intimates no reality of any sort; it is merely a convention for setting out data. There is no doubt that it is based on the order by distance,[17] with precedence given to the Sun and Moon by transposing them to the upper end in acknowledgement of their predominant influence:

Sun Moon Saturn Jupiter Mars Venus Mercury

The horoscopic order carries one very important implication for the Mithraic order. It suggests that the Mithraic order too is in all probability based on the order by distance from the earth; for in the Mithraic order likewise the sequence of the five planets proper remains intact while the two luminaries have been repositioned upwards and together. The horoscopic order shows at least that this was a legitimate and contemporary way of generating a new planetary order. It is thus a reasonable assumption that the Mithraic order was formed on the same principle and from the same original:

horoscopic adaptation

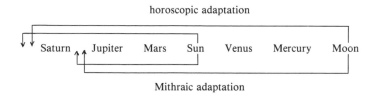

Saturn   Jupiter   Mars   Sun   Venus   Mercury   Moon

Mithraic adaptation

[16] O. Neugebauer and H. B. Van Hoesen, *Greek Horoscopes* (Memoirs of the American Philosophical Society 48, Philadelphia 1959), 164.
[17] Presumably the "Chaldean" version, since Venus is above Mercury; in most attestations of the "Platonic" or "Egyptian" sequence those two planets are reversed.

The Mithraic order, then, as based on the order by distance reflects a spatial reality, not the standard one of the day but one sufficiently close to be recognizable as such. In the undisturbed sequence of the five planets proper the initiate would see an "image of the cosmos"[18] as it extends radially, or "upwards,"[19] from earth to heaven. And given contemporary views on the celestial journey and liberation of the soul, he could not but see his progress through the grades ahead of him, under the successive guardianship of the planets so ordered, as a mimetic traversing of that route through space.[20]

The "Chaldean" order by distance is also the basis for our third important contemporary order, the order of the planets according to the days of the week over which they preside:

Saturn	Sun	Moon	Mars	Mercury	Jupiter	Venus
Saturday	Sunday	Monday	Tuesday	Wednesday	Thursday	Friday

Here no part of the original spatial sequence is left undisturbed. Indeed, the old order is unrecognizable in the new unless one knows the principle of rearrangement, which is the selection of every third planet from the spatial order continuously repeated:

> *Saturn* Jupiter Mars *Sun* Venus Mercury *Moon*
> Saturn Jupiter *Mars* Sun Venus *Mercury* Moon
> Saturn *Jupiter* Mars Sun *Venus* Mercury Moon
> *Saturn* ...

Why the rearrangement was effected in that particular way is not here our concern.[21] What does concern us, though, is that the sequence, in its origin

---

[18] The phrase is from Porphyry's description of the edifice of the mithraeum (*De antro nympharum* 6, trans. of Arethusa edn. [Buffalo 1969]): "This cave [i.e. the archetypal mithraeum] bore for him [sc. Zoroaster, the putative founder of the cult] the image of the cosmos (εἰκόνα κόσμου) which Mithras had created and the things which the cave contained, by their proportionate arrangement, provided him with symbols of the elements and climates of the Cosmos." The grade system and the mithraeum are the two great invented structures of Mithraism. They manifest the same concern with replicating the structure of the macrocosm.

[19] This would be the ancient way of looking at it: a planet's distance is, technically, its "height" (ὕψος).

[20] Obviously relevant here is the testimony of Celsus in Origen *Contra Celsum* 6.22 that the Mithraists had a *symbolon* of a "seven-gated ladder" intimating the passage of the soul through the planetary spheres. This testimony will be discussed in some detail below, as will the scholarly views that lessen its relevance with the argument that it concerns a doctrine of world ages rather than the escape of the soul.

[21] The favoured supposition is that the planets were first assigned not to the days, but to the *hours*. If the hours of the 24-hour *nycthemeris* are repeated and the planets are assigned to them over and over again in the "Chaldean" order, it will be found that if Saturn presides over the first

and derivation from the "Chaldean" order, starts with Saturn and Saturn's day, whatever day of the week subsequently becomes the "first." [22]

The first three days of the planetary week thus belong to Saturn, the Sun and the Moon — in that order. This recalls the summit of the Mithraic *cursus*, and I suggest that the similarity is not accidental. In modifying the classic *spatial* order the Mithraists, I believe, chose for their three highest grades a *temporal* order then coming into vogue.[23] Their *cursus* reflects, then, both of the two universal dimensions, time and space.[24] It is thus truly an "image of the cosmos," a reflection of the world at the highest and most generalized level. To pass through it is to pass through the essentials of the present order.

A structural diagram of the genesis of the Mithraic order from the week-day and "Chaldean" orders reveals two important features:

---

hour of the first day the Sun will preside over the first hour of the second day, the Moon over the first hour of the third day, and so on, until the return of Saturn as the power of the first hour of the eighth day or of the first day of a new "week." The *locus classicus* on this is Cassius Dio 37.18. The excellent monograph of F. H. Colson, *The Week; An Essay on the Origin and Development of the Seven-Day Cycle* (Cambridge 1926 [rp. Westport, Conn., 1974]), contains the essential information on the planetary week. See also Boll (above, n. 7), 2556-61, 2570-77; P. Brind'Amour, *Le Calendrier romain* (Coll. d'études anc. de L'Univ. d'Ottawa 2, Ottawa 1983), 256-268; R. Merkelbach, *Mithras* (above, n. 4), 212 f.

[22] Boll (above, n. 7), 2577. The primacy of Saturn and Saturn's day were reinforced by the assimilation of the planetary week to the more ancient Jewish week and of Saturn's day to the sabbath; see Colson (preceding note), 11-17, 39-61.

[23] There are references to the planetary week, both literary and epigraphical, contemporary with or earlier than what I take to be the cult's formative years early in the second century A.D.: Boll (above, n. 7), 2573 ff., Colson (above, n. 21), 14-38. "Die Ausbreitung der Planetenwoche im Bereiche der griechisch-römischen Kultur können wir erst von der Zeit des Kaisers Augustus an verfolgen" (Boll 2573); "... the planetary week was known in some sense in the Empire as early as the destruction of Pompeii and most people will think a century earlier" (Colson 36). Colson, however, cautions against supposing that the planetary week was universally current even in the second century: "Justin [*Ap.* 1.67] is perhaps the earliest writer who assumes that the casual reader will understand the week without explanation" (*ibid.*). The week-day order of the planets was of course also known and used by the Mithraists. The monuments and the passage of Origen *Contra Celsum* which attest it will be discussed below. Dating by the day of the week is found within the cult in an important graffito in the Sa. Prisca Mithraeum (*CIMRM* 498: *Natus prima luce / duobus Augg. cos. / Severo et Anton(ino) / XII K(al.) Decem(bres) / dies Saturni / luna XVIII* (i.e. Saturday, 20 November, A.D. 202). M. Guarducci has argued (correctly, in my view) that it is the Mithras of this particular mithraeum who is "born" on the date celebrated and that the graffito is thus the horoscope, as it were, and dedicatory inscription of the mithraeum: "Il graffito *Natus prima luce* nel mitreo di S. Prisca," *Mysteria Mithrae*, 153-163. If that is so, the fact that Saturn's day was chosen is probably of some significance.

[24] In the two sentences in which he alludes to it, Flamant characterizes the Mithraic grade order in essentially the same way as a conflation of the week-day order at the top and the spatial order at the bottom (*art. cit.* [above, n. 7], 230): "on trouve même parfois une série qui commence par l'ordre hebdomadaire (Saturne, Sol, Luna) et se termine par l'ordre céleste (Jupiter, Mars, Vénus, Mercure), ordre initiatique."

GRADES   ORDERS

| | | Temporal | Mithraic | Spatial |
		(week-day)		('Chaldean')
Pater	↑	Saturn ⟶	Saturn ⟵	Saturn
Heliodromus		Sun ⟶	Sun	
Perses		Moon ⟶	Moon	
Leo			Jupiter ⟵	Jupiter
Miles			Mars ⟵	Mars
Nymphus			Venus ⟵	Venus
Corax			Mercury ⟵	Mercury

First, Saturn is the only planet to appear in the relevant parts of both contributing orders and is set at the summit of the Mithraic order by virtue of his
position in both the temporal and spatial sequences. The Pater, who is *tutela
Saturni*, is thus appropriately the master of the ends of both time and space.
Nama patribus ab oriente ad occidentem tutela Saturni, as the Santa Prisca
dipinto proclaims: the glory of the Fathers, under the protection of Saturn, is
to extend from east to west which are the boundaries of the world and from
sunrise to sunset which are the boundaries of the day.

Secondly, the progress through the grades of initiation, while it corresponds
spatially to a progress "up" or outwards from earth through the spheres of
the planets, corresponds temporally to a progress *backwards* — as it were,
from Monday to Sunday to Saturday. The spatial progress is not particularly
surprising. It is of course significant that the motion is upwards and outwards,
but it could, without paradox, have been in the opposite direction. In space,
after all, we can move either forwards or backwards, provided that there is no
physical constraint either way. But to move backwards in time is an im-
possibility — at least in the "real" world — and to set up a progress with that
connotation is to assert a paradox, something on the face of it nonsensical or
perverse. It is as if one were to say to the initiates of the upper grades (whom it
seems exclusively to concern), "If today you are a Heliodromus, tomorrow
you were a Perses and yesterday you will be a Pater."[25]

Paradox and "nonsense" are never far from the surface of the Mysteries of
Mithras. For a comparable enigma one need look no further than the name of
one of the grades, the Nymphus, which, as R. L. Gordon has rightly

---

[25] A nice example of the effect of this enigma when it is not consciously faced can be seen in
Flamant's description of the grade structure quoted in the preceding note. Flamant's analysis into
the two contributing orders is correct and perceptive, but assuming — as we naturally do — that
time runs forward, he begins at the top end of the progression through the grades — and so
asserts a manifest untruth: the "order of initiation" does not "commence" with the week-day
order (Saturn, Sol, Luna) and "end" with the spatial order (Jupiter, Mars, Venus, Mercury), *but
precisely the other way round*. If one is to be true to the logic of the Mysteries, one must be
prepared on occasions to suspend the logic of our normal world and to entertain such absurdities
as a reversal of the flow of time.

stressed,[26] is a non-word for an impossible thing — a male bride. As always, the paradox is designed to make a serious point, and to make it economically and strikingly. In the present instance it is not hard to see what that point is, for it is clearly analogous to the point made by the upwards and outwards progress in the spatial sequence. Just as the progress through the lower grades is a miming of a journey up and out through the planetary spheres and thus as an escape from and a triumphing over the spatial constraints of mortality, so the progress through the three higher grades represents liberation from and victory over the other dimension of our mortal life, time as symbolized in the planetary week. In advancing from Monday to Sunday to Saturday the initiate defies time's one-way rule and so annuls its tyranny over him.

The comparison of the Mithraic grade order with the other planetary orders then current has led to the conclusion — necessarily tentative, as most findings about the Mysteries inevitably are — that the Mithraic order was generated by conflating the week-day order with the standard "Chaldean" order of the planets by distance; further, that its structure shows it to be a microcosmic enactment of a macrocosmic journey through space and time which enables the initiate to triumph over both dimensions and to win his freedom from the material universe which they define. The new order is thus seen to be a masterly adaptation which allowed the Mysteries to exploit to the utmost the spatial and temporal symbolism inherent in planetary sequences. On the one hand, it validates the progress through the grades as a journey through space and time far more effectively than could any of the existing orders alone. It thus carries the authority of a uniquely accurate and comprehensive map for those who would undertake that journey. This is exactly what one would expect of the claims to wisdom and competence of an esoteric cult: our road is a better road because we alone know the true structure of the universe and can guide you though it. On the other hand, the Mysteries did not make the mistake of breaking entirely with the old orders. The new order is not an outrageous novelty, linked with nothing in the world outside, whose claims would seem ill-founded and alarming. It does not deny the other orders or the profane learning and common knowledge behind them; rather, it perfects and fulfils them: this is the road which you have known all along, but which is now revealed to you — the elect — as it really is.

III

The second line of enquiry which I proposed at the outset was to look at other orderings of the planets found within Mithraism. Explicitly, at least, such instances do not concern the grades, but we should nevertheless be alert to the

---

[26] (above, n. 4), 48 ff.

possibility of resonances between the overtly expressed order — whatever than happens to be — and the grade sequence. In at least one instance, the important testimonium of Celsus in Origen *Contra Celsum* 6.22 (to be discussed at the end), I am convinced that such resonances exist and indeed that the testimonium adds credibility to the interpretation of the grade structure as a model of the cosmos in traversing which the initiate wins his freedom. In any case, the exploration of the use of other orders in the cult is worth-while in itself; among other things, it will open up the possibility of some remarkable new meanings in the tauroctony, the scene of Mithras killing the bull which is the principal icon of the Mysteries. We shall find, too, that the deployment of planetary orders is very much more varied, subtle, and "scientific," especially in the exploitation of the categories of learned astrology, than has been suspected.

Apart from the Celsus testimonium, the evidence all comes from the cult's monuments. Representations of groups of seven stars or seven altars are common enough,[27] especially on tauroctonies, and obviously denote the seven planets — and perhaps through their tutelary powers the grades too. But since the objects are undifferentiated, they can tell us nothing — as yet — about planetary orders; only that the collectivity of the planets is somehow implicated in the central act which the icon portrays. Only on the monument of Ottaviano Zeno, as we shall see, and perhaps also on the Barberini fresco, is there a possibility of deciphering a sequence from the undifferentiated row of altars by means of its concomitants. This leaves, then, a relatively few monuments on which the planets are individually identifiable in the figures or busts of their deities and in which an order can accordingly be determined. However, one of these, *CIMRM* 693, will be found to provide a key of sorts to the significance of the anonymous row of altars above the scene of the tauroctony.

IV

In two instances, images of the planetary gods appear in mosaic on the benches or floors of mithraea. These are the Ostian mithraea, Sette Sfere and

---

[27] Seven stars: in the field of the bull-killing scene, e.g. *CIMRM* 368; on Mithras' billowing cloak (thus signifying that the garment is the cosmos of which he is creator or controller), e.g. 390. Seven altars: e.g. 2264, and see the indices of *CIMRM* (both vols) *s.* "altar — seven." The monuments in which the altars are set in a row between Sol and Luna will be discussed below. Occasionally, as in 670, trees or daggers/swords alternate with the altars. The most complex relief in this respect is 1973 (Apulum), where we find, alternating with seven altars in a row extending between Sol and Luna, eight sets of symbols, each set consisting of (l. to r.) a cap on a stick, a tree, and a dagger, except for (i) the set on the far left — tree and dagger only, (ii) the second set from the left — cap with stick and dagger only, and (iii) the group on the far right — cap with stick and tree only. The number seven, so the scholium on Plato *Alcibiades* I 121E (= *TMMM* 2.54) tells us, was considered "proper" (οἰκεῖον) to Mithras.

Sette Porte.[28] They have in common the fact that only six of the seven planets
are represented. The missing planet is the Sun. Since his omission is so
paradoxical in the context of a mithraeum, one conjectures that he is in fact
present though in another guise — as the Sol-Mithras of the tauroctony in the
cult-niche. Arguably, too, the dispositions of the planetary symbols in the two
mithraea are variants of each other,[29] the cross-wise pairings at Sette Sfere
corresponding to lengthwise at Sette Porte:

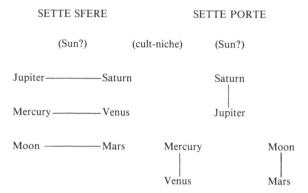

   SETTE SFERE   SETTE PORTE

    (Sun?)   (cult-niche)   (Sun?)

   Jupiter———————Saturn   Saturn

   Mercury———————Venus   Jupiter

   Moon ————————Mars Mercury   Moon

            Venus   Mars

These dispositions, not to mention the reduction — at least explicitly — to a
set of six, are without parallel whether within or outside the Mysteries. Furthermore, unlike the Mithraic grade order, they cannot convincingly be shown
to derive from any known planetary sequence.[30] However, I shall not analyse
them here, since I have argued elsewhere that they represent and celebrate actual, rather striking configurations of the planets relative to the Sun at the
time of the spring equinox in A.D. 172 and again in 173,[31] and to the best of
my knowledge there is no other current theory to account for them except simple aberration.[32] If I am correct, the arrangements are specific to particular

---

[28] The *CIMRM* numbers of the mithraea are 239 ff. (Sette Sfere) and 287 ff. (Sette Porte); of
their planetary symbols, respectively 241 and 288. I exclude from consideration the Spoleto
Mithraeum (673 ff., 677) which certainly had the planetary gods painted on the side-benches.
However, since only two of the figures were preserved, it is impossible to reconstruct their
sequence.

[29] Appreciated by R. L. Gordon in "The Sacred Geography of a *Mithraeum*: The Example of
Sette Sfere," *JMS* 1 (1976), 119-165, at 140, though from a faulty perspective (see below, n. 32).

[30] Bianchi, *Mysteria Mithrae* 32-38, esp. 34 f., does derive them from the week-day order. But I
believe that the actual arrangements in the mithraea (especially in Sette Porte where Bianchi ad-
mits that the order is "heavily perturbed and [almost] destroyed") would not be recognizable as
variants of the week-day order. Moreover, a motive for the distortion of an original week-day
order is not readily discernible: why, in other words, would the designer(s) have first selected the
week-day order and then scrambled it? See my criticisms in "Sette Sfere, Sette Porte, and the
Spring Equinoxes of A.D. 172 and 173," *Mysteria Mithrae* 515-530, at 526-529.

[31] In the article cited in the preceding note.

[32] Richard Gordon tells me that he no longer holds the theory, advanced in his article on the
two mithraea ([above, n. 29], 140 f.), that the arrangement has to do with the *thema mundi*; see
my "Sette Sfere ..." (above, n. 30), 516 f.

mithraea and particular celestial events and so can tell us nothing general about Mithraic doctrine on the planets, their ordering or their relation to the grades, although the implications for the Mysteries' concern with the actualities of astronomy, including the ephemera of planetary longitudes, are of some significance.[33] One point should, however, be made. Apart from the images of the individual deities, the planets are also collectively represented in both mithraea by the symbols which have given the mithraea their modern names: the seven arcs set one above another up the aisle of Sette Sfere, and the arcade of six arches with the large central gate as a seventh in Sette Porte. Potentially, these offer alternative planetary orders to that fixed in each mithraeum by the images of the gods. For they share a strange but easily overlooked feature: both sets are empty — empty arcs and empty archways. They therefore hint at different possibilities for their filling; just as an empty chess board hints at innumerable particular games of chess, so these empty arches hint at other planetary orders germane to the Mysteries in addition to the local and very specific sequence published in each mithraeum by the images of the gods. At Sette Porte the prominent central arch and gateway suggest the Sun at the mid point of the universe, with three planets above and three below. The arcade as a whole thus seems to imply the "Chaldean" order of the planets by distance from the earth, of which the central Sun is the distinctive feature (see above, p. 6). Sette Sfere is more open, in the sense that the seven arcs are utterly undifferentiated. In imagination, then, or by mimesis — by the setting out and interchange of moveable images or of the initiates themselves as actors — the seven "spheres" could be transformed into any or every planetary sequence, including of course that of the grades. A third monument, though of a much later date (late fourth century), was almost certainly used for such a purpose. It is *CIMRM* 399/406, a marble block of about two meters by a half, from the Mithraeum of S. Silvestro in Capite. The front was carved into a row of seven niches, in which, it is assumed, images of the planetary gods were displayed. It is noteworthy that the dedicator draws attention to his family's devotion not only to Mithras but also to the heavens and the stars; for he speaks of his grandfather, the founder of the mithraeum, as *caelo devotus et astris*.[34]

---

[33] The theory acquires, I believe, some credibility from what are arguably similar instances of the incorporation of astronomical data in the foundation of other mithraea: see above, n. 23, on Guarducci's theory of the *natus prima luce* ... graffito as, in effect, the horoscope of the Sa. Prisca Mithraeum; also the Postscript to my "Interpreting the Ponza Zodiac, II," *JMS* 2 (1978), 87-147, at 135 f., on that monument as a commemoration of the solar eclipse of 14 August, A.D. 212.

[34] On this monument see D. Gallo, "Il mitreo di S. Silvestro in Capite," *Mysteria Mithrae* 231-247, with plates. A similar use was made, I believe, of the furniture of the recently discovered Vulci Mithraeum. The benches there are carried on arches, six on each side forming a series of niches. The suggestion that they were identified with the twelve signs of the zodiac (Gordon in a comment on A. M. Sgubini Moretti, "Nota preliminare su un mitreo scoperto a Vulci," *Mysteria*

V

Busts of the seven planetary gods set in a row are found on two representations of the bull-killing, and probably also on a third.[35] In the two certain in-

---

Mithrae 259-277, at 277) is surely correct. But one may speculate further that images of the planets could also be placed in the niches and moved so as to replicate actual planetary positions or to set the planets in other significant relationships as desired. The mithraeum could thus be transformed into a true and precise "image of the heavens." The small statue of Cautes found in this mithraeum is also of interest here (Sgubini Moretti 273 f. with Pls. 11 and 12). On its back are carved seven arcs one below the other. Superficially, these are folds in the floor-length cloak; but their regularity and their unnaturalness in an otherwise naturalistic sculpture indicate that more is intended: in fact, the seven planetary spheres — as at Sette Sfere.

[35] The probable third is *CIMRM* 1271, a fragment from the upper right corner of a relief found in the Dieburg Mithraeum. Preserved are a row of four busts of which the left one (approximately at the centre of the relief's upper border) is virtually obliterated. If they are indeed planetary gods and if, as seems most likely, the three better preserved ones on the right are all male, then the sequence was probably that of the order by distance ending with Mars, Jupiter and Saturn. This would make for a most interesting composition, in that the Sun would be in the centre — as we saw, the principal feature that recommended this order in general — directly above the bull-killing Mithras, while the Moon would be on the extreme left. Presumably, there would also have been the usual busts of Sol and Luna within the scene of the bull-killing itself, with Sol on the left in contrast to the Moon in the planetary sequence above, and Luna on the right in contrast to Saturn above. Alternatively, if the bust on the extreme right of the planetary sequence is not male, it would probably be the Moon's and the sequence would be that of the days of the week running from right to left. The next figure from the right is bearded and would be Mars, while the third is youngish and would fit well with Mercury. The composition would then be the same as that of the Bologna relief (see below) and its logic would (as there) be the arrangement of the planetary gods in a sequence which puts the Moon in her usual place in the upper right corner of a tauroctony and the Sun in the upper left. On this reconstruction there would of course be no additional Sol and Luna lower down. R. Merkelbach (*Mithras* [above, n. 4], 356, Abb. 119) rightly suggests yet another possibility: (r. to l.) Venus, Jupiter, Mercury, Mars. This yields the week-day order, starting on the far left (lost) with Saturn, in an arrangement identical with that of the Brigetio plate (see below).

I also exclude from further consideration *CIMRM* 1475, a relief from Siscia. In one of the scenes at the top of its circular border, a row of seven altars is surmounted by three gods, (l. to r.) Mercury, Jupiter, Mars. The sequence of the three corresponds neither to that in the "Chaldean" order, not to that in the week-day order, nor to that in the Mithraic grade order. Furthermore, since the gods are not individually related to particular altars, it seems that no particular planetary order is intimated. Rather, Jupiter is in the centre of the trio simply as occupying the position of honour.

Also excluded here are those other monuments from the frontier provinces on which a group of gods, of varying number, is represented usually full figure as in *CIMRM* 1475 but without altars in their immediate vicinity. In most instances the identities of one or more of the gods are in doubt since the figures are generally small, crude and badly worn; only in a single instance is there unquestionably a set of seven; and always there is doubt as to whether *planetary* gods are intended rather than (e.g.) a selection of Olympians. For completeness' sake, I comment briefly on the monuments of this type listed by Merkelback (p. 208, n. 46) with the claim that they carry figures of some or all the planetary gods. (Strangely, Merkelbach omits 1475 itself, as also the Sette Porte figures.) (1) *CIMRM* 1128: Three gods in centre of upper register: Merkelbach lists as (l. to r.) Mercury, Mars, Jupiter; Vermaseren (*CIMRM* description) as Mercury, Mars, Saturn. Saturn seems to me more probable as the god on the right since there are indications of a veil in the photograph. (2) 1137: This highly unusual monument has on its obverse four upper registers one above the other. Merkelbach identifies the two figures on the right of the third register (from the top) and the four on the left of the fourth register as the planetary gods: (l. to r.) Mars, Venus;

stances, as in the testimonium of Celsus, the order is that of the days of the week. This means that the classic order by distance is nowhere indubitably attested in the Mysteries in its unmodified form. This is somewhat surprising, since it is the commonest in the outside world and, as we have seen, forms the basis of the other major orders. In so far, then, as one may generalize from so tiny a sample, the emphasis of planetary symbolism in the Mysteries seems to be on time rather than space.

Saturn, Jupiter, Sun, Moon, Mercury. Apart from the fact that the figures are divided between two registers and thus are not, at least demonstrably, a single set, the identities of three of them are by no means certain. "Mars" and "Venus," by themselves on the third register, are merely male and female figures without attributes, the former grasping the latter by the hair (why?): "Mercury" has only an indistinct object held in his raised left hand (his purse?). The figures *might*, then, represent the full complement of planetary gods, but not certainly and not as a set. If they do, the order is inexplicable except in terms of natural pairings: Mars with Venus, Saturn with Jupiter (the transfer of the thunderbolt is shown), and Sol with Luna; Mercury is then the "odd man out." (3) 1430: The upper right panel of this relief from Virunum shows a row of five seated gods of whom the one on the far left is almost all lost and the next partially so; in the panel below are two reclining deities, one male and the other female. Merkelbach identifies the upper five as (l. to r.) Sun, Moon, Jupiter, Mars, Mercury, the lower two as Venus and Saturn. Vermaseren (*CIMRM* description) finds in the upper panel Mercury (?), Mars (?), Jupiter, Juno, Minerva. There is agreement, then, only on Jupiter. On photographs the two figures on the right do seem to be female. On the lower panel the reclining god can only be identified as Saturn by ignoring, as Merkelbach does, the fact that he wears horns! I would suggest, then, that he is a river god representing the element of water, as his female partner represents earth. Vermaseren sees here Oceanus and a Nereid. The likelihood that these two panels carry the seven planetary gods is negligible. (4) 1797: In this fragment from an upper right corner Merkelbach finds three of the planets: Moon, Saturn, Venus. Actually, the Moon is the usual Luna of the tauroctony, Saturn is the reclining figure of the normal side-scene (the dreaming Saturn), and "Venus" is an indistinct bust which Vermaseren (*CIMRM* description) describes as capped and possibly a season. There is no reason to suppose that the other four planets might have appeared below in the lost part of the relief. (5) 2202: Four gods appear at the apex of the upper register. Merkelbach does not identify them. Vermaseren sees them as Minerva, Jupiter, Mercury and Mars (l. to r.). (6) 2338: There are three gods in the centre of the upper register: (l. to r.) Mercury, Mars, Jupiter. Vermaseren gives the same identities, but from autopsy it seems to me that the "shield" of "Mars" may equally well be a cloak and that his "lance" is too thick to represent that object. By including Sol and Luna at either extreme and the dreaming Saturn below the latter, Merkelbach finds six of the seven planetary gods — Venus alone is missing. There are, however, several other scenes intervening in this crowded upper register, and the likelihood that the six gods present in various places there are intended as a planetary set is minimal. (7) 2340: Although Merkelbach suggests only a possibility here, this fragment is perhaps the most interesting monument in that it does offer indisputably a row of seven gods. Merkelbach suggests (l. to r.) Saturn, Luna, Venus (?), Mercury (?), Jupiter, Sol, Mars; Vermaseren suggests Neptune (with trident), Luna, Juno, Minerva (in helmet), Jupiter, Sol, Mars. There is obviously, then, no certainty that the seven are the planetary set. If they are, the order is incomprehensible. Interestingly, while the other gods appear full figure, Luna and Sol are represented as busts.

    Finally, I exclude — though for very different reasons — *CIMRM* 307. This Ostian monument consists of two fragments, one found *near* the Sabazeo Mithraeum, of a frieze of the heads of the planetary gods. Here there is no uncertainty as to the planets' identity; the question is rather whether the monument is actually Mithraic. The order is that of the days of the week beginning with Saturn on the left. The arrangement is the same as on the Brigetio plate (see below), with which 307, if Mithraic, should accordingly be classed.

The two tauroctonies on which the busts of the seven planetary gods definitely appear in the week-day order are (i) *CIMRM* 693, a relief of Danubian provenance (or antecedents), until a few years ago in Bologna, and (ii) 1727, a bronze plate from Brigetio in Pannonia. The authenticity of a part of the Bologna relief with some of the planetary busts has recently been called in question. This problem I have delayed to an Appendix. Even if the part at issue is a modern restoration, the order of the planets in the original is reasonably secure. Consequently, what follows can be accepted with confidence, except of course in the very few places where the iconography of certain of the individual planets is concerned. However, as I argue in the Appendix, there is good reason to accept the part as genuine and original. If it is not, then, in particular, my exploration of the significance of the iconography of the central bust (pp. 32-34) must be discounted. Fortunately, that exploration is marginal to the main line of my interpretation of the planetary series.

On the Bologna relief the planets are set in an arc above the scene, running from the Moon on the right to the Sun on the left:

←———————————————————————————————————

Sun   Saturn   Venus   Jupiter   Mercury   Mars   Moon

The order appears to be determined by the conceit of making the Sun and Moon do double duty both as members of the planetary set of seven and as the regular pair found in the upper left and upper right corners of the stereotype of the tauroctony.[36] Given, then, that the other planets must be spread between the Sun on the left and the Moon on the right, the only order in which they can appear (other than in haphazard distribution) is that of the days of the week, and necessarily the sequence must start with the Moon and run leftwards — if it is to be read in temporal sequence. It would be tempting to see in this reversed direction an allusion to the breaking of time which I have argued we find in the grade order. But if there is such an allusion, it cannot be shown to be more than a fortunate consequence of the conceit which is the primary determinant of the composition. The same, indeed, is true of the choice of the week-day order itself: it follows from the choice of the positioning of Sun and Moon and is thus secondary.[37] The order on the second monument, the

---

[36] A similar conceit is found in the relief from Sidon (*CIMRM* 75), where the scorpion who is regularly set at the bull's genitals also serves as the Scorpius of the surrounding zodiac.

[37] Secondary, too, must be the consideration, suggested by Bianchi, of giving the Sun the "primacy" ([above, n. 5], 34). Essentially, the Sun is where he is on the far left because that is Sol's usual place in the tauroctony. The same limitation applies to Cumont's suggestion that the sequence, "inverse de celle qu'on attendrait, fait peut-être allusion au mouvement rétrograde des astres errants, qui a provoqué dans l'antiquité tant de commentaires" (*TMMM* 1.114). Given that "Monday" must be on the right and "Sunday" on the left, the only route between them which covers the days in between lies leftwards. Actually, Cumont's suggestion is implausible in itself,

Brigetio plate, is not similarly constrained. Here the planets are found below the main scene, from Saturn on the left to Venus on the right:

Saturn　Sun　Moon　Mars　Mercury　Jupiter　Venus
————————————————————————————————→

It may be that the designer chose the week-day order commencing with Saturn partly in order to evoke the upper end of the grade order (Saturn, Sun, Moon); partly, too, to emphasize the primacy of Saturn,[38] above even the Sun and the Moon and separated from the other planets proper by the luminaries, a feature which the week-day order so displayed shares with the Mithraic grade order. But it is possible that no such ulterior motives are at work. The order and its starting point are unexceptional and so require no special explanation. Perhaps no more was intended than a display of the planetary powers in a mode which would emphasize time and so complement the other set of temporal symbols, the busts of the seasons in the scene's four corners.

While admitting of the Bologna relief that the design of fitting the planets between Sol and Luna is sufficient to explain their sequence and that no further consideration need necessarily have played a part, we are entitled to ask the anterior question of what determines the positions of Sol and Luna respectively on the left and right of the scene of the tauroctony. That is, of course, a question which concerns the composition of the icon in general, not merely the Bologna exemplar.[39] And at first sight it might seem a rather unpromising question, for why should the placing of the Sun on the left and the Moon on the right be other than an arbitrary choice in the composition? What, moreover, could it have to do with the set of the seven planets and their

---

for the retrograde motion of the planets is westward and according to the usual system of ancient astronomical alignment westward motion is motion from left to right. The suggestion can, however, be salvaged by construing the direction of the sequence on the Bologna relief as an allusion to the eastward, and hence leftward, motion which the planets *generally* pursue — retrograde motion is intermittent and in any case does not apply to the Sun or Moon — and which notoriously is in contrary sense to the westward motion "of the universe," i.e. of all celestial bodies daily. I have argued elsewhere ("Cautes and Cautopates: Some Astronomical Considerations," *JMS* 2 [1977] 1-19, at 9 f.) that the icon of the tauroctony is in fact oriented after the pattern of the heavens with east to the left of the composition and west to the right. On that supposition, to read the sequence of the planets in the week-day order from right to left, as we find them on the Bologna relief, is indeed to follow them in the direction of their distinctive motion.

[38] To this theme we shall return. It is that rightly stressed by Bianchi (above, n. 5). Merkelbach (*Mithras* [above, n. 4], 209) unaccountably describes the order as "beginnend mit dem Tag des Sonnengottes und endend mit dem Tag des Saturn;" hence, quite mistakenly, "hier hat Sol die Vorrangstellung."

[39] The disposition of Sol and Luna to the left and right respectively is a norm which is contravened on very few monuments. L. A. Campbell (*Mithraic Iconography and Ideology* [EPRO 11, Leiden 1968], 137) lists only eight examples, to which *CIMRM* 1468 should be added as a ninth.

disposition or sequence? Nevertheless, as I shall try to demonstrate, the question is both relevant and revealing.

The busts of the planetary gods are not the only feature in the Bologna relief additional to the regular set of components which make up the bull-killing scene. Certain rare, though not unique, details have been added in the vicinity of the torchbearers. It is, of course, usual for the scene to be flanked by these two figures, Cautes on one side with his raised torch and Cautopates on the other with his lowered torch. This we find in the Bologna relief, and following the pattern of Danubian monuments Cautes is placed on the right and Cautopates on the left.[40] However, in addition to their torches, the two figures are associated with secondary attributes: a bull's head is set in the field next to Cautes and a scorpion next to Cautopates.[41] These secondary attributes are found in a few other monuments of the cult, on both tauroctonies and free-standing individual statues of the torch-bearers.[42]

The bull's head and the scorpion introduce those other celestial beings which share the heavens with the planets, namely the stars and constellations — and in particular those twelve constellations which, as the signs of the zodiac, are especially related to the planets as markers of their path around the celestial sphere.[43] For, as is generally agreed, the bull's head symbolizes

---

[40] Danubian provenance — or a Danubian model — is suggested primarily by the sequence of three subsidiary scenes in a lower register. These, however, are in some respects different from their normal Danubian types: three figures (rather than the customary two) reclining at the banquet, and no two of them clearly identifiable as Sol and Mithras; a winged putto — so it seemed to me on autopsy (also Brizzolara [(below, n. 240), 99], but see *CIMRM*)—ascending in the horse-drawn biga instead of Sol and Mithras; the dreaming Saturn (surely this rather than "Ocean," as *CIMRM* and Brizzolara) in place of the usual snake-entwined figure reclining but with raised arm. *Adaptation* of a Danubian model is thus perhaps the more likely alternative.

[41] There is also a tree in the field on each side. On inspection, I could not detect any real difference between the two, although Campbell ([above, n. 39], 26) and Vermaseren ([below, n. 49], 37) assert (as did Cumont [*TMMM* 1.211], though with reservations) that the tree on the left (with Cautopates and the scorpion) has fruit while that on the right (with Cautes and the bull's head) is barren.

[42] For a list of the monuments and an analysis, see my "Cautes and Cautopates ..." (above, n. 37), 3 f.; also Vermaseren (below, n. 49), 37 ff. It is analogy with those other monuments that makes me accept that Cautes' "bull's head" on the Bologna relief really is such. Certainly, it has always been so identified, but I must admit that on autopsy it seemed to me more like a lion's mask. Brizzolara ([below, n. 240], 97) reports a bull's head, perhaps influenced by the received description since she does so without qualification. There is a similar problem with the bull's head in the recently discovered tauroctony of the Ottaviano Zeno relief (see below, n. 50).

[43] For our purposes, the constellations of the zodiac and the signs of the zodiac can be treated as equivalent. In fact, the constellations are the actual groups or patterns of stars, while the signs are the twelve equal arcs into which the circle of the zodiac is divided and which, in antiquity at least, were occupied (with more or less accurate fit) by the twelve constellations. The planets move (generally) eastward around the zodiac (see above, n. 37) in their respective periods (Moon — 1 month; Sun with Mercury and Venus — 1 year; Mars — approx. 2 years; Jupiter — approx. 12 years; Saturn — approx. 29 years). The Sun moves on the ecliptic which is the central line of the zodiac; the other planets wander to the north and south of the ecliptic but always within the band of the zodiac.

the constellation and sign of Taurus and the scorpion the constellation and sign of Scorpius.[44] Now Taurus and Scorpius occupy diametrically opposite positions on the celestial sphere and on the zodiac, and part of the purpose of assigning their symbols to Cautes and Cautopates is to signify that the scene whose margins the torchbearers define corresponds to that semicircle of the zodiac, that half of the heavens, which lies between those two signs. As I have argued before, the tauroctony is celestially aligned, corresponding to a view of the heavens by a south-facing observer, so that west is to the right of the scene and east to the left.[45] Accordingly, if the bull's head is set on the right and the scorpion on the left, this signifies that Taurus is in the west while Scorpius is in the east, and the visible semicircle which extends across the heavens in between is that occupied by the sequence of signs Taurus-Gemini-Cancer-Leo-Virgo-Libra-Scorpius (see diagram, fig. 1). It is of course no accident that that semicircle possesses, in itself or as paranatellonta, constellations which are the counterparts of virtually all the components, regular or occasional, of the tauroctony:[46]

Taurus	the bull
Canis Major ⎱ Canis Minor ⎰	the dog
Hydra	the snake
Crater	the cup or bowl
Leo	the lion
Spica (Alpha Virginis)	the wheat ear(s) at the tip of the bull's tail
Corvus	the raven
Scorpius	the scorpion

---

[44] See, e.g., Cumont *TMMM* 1.210 f. As far as I know, these correspondences have never been denied. The fullest treatment is my own: *art. cit.* (above, n. 37). The identification of the torch-bearers with Taurus and Scorpius also have seasonal implications, but these do not concern us here. However, since they have been widely misinterpreted, I would refer the reader to p. 5 of my article.

[45] *Art. cit.* 8 ff.; and see above, n. 37. In my article, I suggest that the tauroctony is to be construed within the Romans religious tradition as a *templum* in the primacy sense of that word, i.e. a ritual quartering of the heavens for observation.

[46] The point is made in my article (above, n. 37), p. 10; subsequently by S. Insler, "A New Interpretation of the Bull-Slaying Motif," in M. B. de Boer and T. A. Edridge (edd.), *Hommages à Maarten J. Vermaseren* (Leiden 1978), 519-538. The correspondences are also used by M. P. Speidel, *Mithras-Orion: Greek Hero and Roman Army God* (EPRO 81, Leiden 1980), though for the purpose of effecting an equation — unwarranted, in my view (see my review, *Phoenix* 36 [1982] 196-198) — between the tauroctonous Mithras and the constellation of Orion.

The paranatellonta are those constellations which lie to the north or south of the zodiac — in the present instance, all to the south — and which "rise alongside" the signs of the zodiac. They are hence, in a sense, surrogates of the zodiacal signs or constellations. Lists of them can be found, e.g., in Aratus (559-732) and Manilius (5.32-709).

What, though, has this to do with the planets, in particular with the planets as ordered on the Bologna relief? For the answer one must turn to astrology. Of fundamental importance in that art are the constantly changing positions of the planets on the zodiac. To make their predictions in a systematic way, the astrologers had to establish sets of relationships between the planets and the signs of the zodiac which would determine by agreed convention where and in what way each planet would exercise its special influence. Essentially, this was a matter of assigning, arbitrarily and according to various patterns, particular planets to particular signs or subdivisions of signs.[47] That, at any rate, was the necessary first stage in the process. One of the schemes of relating planets and signs — there are others which we shall need to consider later — was to assign the former to *thirds* of the latter. Each sign, in other words, was divided into three sections and the planets were distributed to them sequentially. These sections were called decans, since each is 10° in length.[48] As units, they were not fashioned *de novo* for this purpose, but rather adapted from an earlier use in Egyptian astronomy where they had served as a series of 36 constellations whose successive risings at 10-day intervals had marked the course of the year. The planets were assigned to the decans (or the decans to the planets) in the order of the planet's distance from the earth (the "Chaldean" order), but beginning with Mars rather than Saturn. Mars was assigned to the first decan of the first sign, which for this purpose (as often in other contexts) was Aries, the sign of the spring equinox. The Sun thus acquires the second decan of Aries, Venus the third, Mercury the first decan of Taurus, and so on (see diagram, fig. 1). Technically, the decan was known as the "mask" (πρόσωπον/*facies*) of its planet. That was because each decan retained, from its Egyptian original, a divine form (frequently theriomorphic), and the planet appears there in that particular guise.

A consequence of assigning the planets by order of distance to successive *thirds* of the signs is that the planets will be distributed to the first, second or third decans of successive signs in the order of the days of the week. For, as we have seen (above, p. 8), the week-day order itself is generated from the order by distance by the successive selection of every *third* planet from the latter order repeated as necessary. Thus, for example, the first decan of Aries belongs to Mars (Tuesday), the first of Taurus to Mercury (Wednesday), the

---

[47] The arbitrary quality of the relationships should be noted. There is of course no real link between signs and planets, except in the case of the Sun whose passage from sign to sign does indeed mark the course of the year and the different seasons. Inevitably, though, the fertile mind of astrology invented justifications. For example, the system of planetary "houses" (see below) was warranted by the *thema mundi*, the horoscope of the universe which held that the planets had each occupied his or her (diurnal) house at the moment of creation.

[48] I.e. one thirty-sixth (3 × 12) of the full 360° circle of the zodiac. On the decans in general see Bouché-Leclercq (above, n. 7), 215-233.

first of Gemini to Jupiter (Thursday), and so on. The decanate, then, with a certain elegant simplicity, involves both of the great orders, that of time as well as that of space.

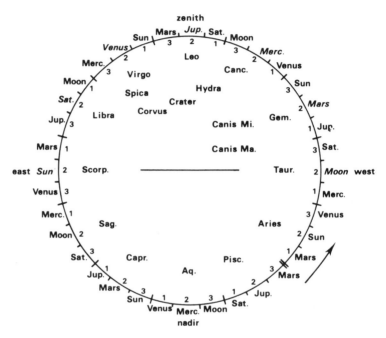

Fig. 1 *The tauroctony and the decans*

The circle of the zodiac is here set with Taurus on the right in the west and Scorpius on the left in the east; Leo is at the zenith. This is the position intimated, on the hypothesis of this study, in the tauroctony. The constellations to the south of the zodiac (paranatellonta) which have counterparts in the tauroctony have been placed very approximately (since this is a diagram, not a chart). The beginning — and end — of the sequence of decans at the spring equinox is marked with a double line (Mars has both the first decan of Aries and the last of Pisces) and its direction by an arrow. The gods of the second, i.e. the central, decans of the signs from Taurus to Scorpius are italicized. They follow the sequence of the days of the week from the Moon on the right across to the Sun on the left — precisely their setting in the Bologna relief (*CIMRM* 693).

We are now in a position to see the appropriateness — to use no other term — of the planetary lay-out across the top of the Bologna relief. The scene below alludes to the span of the zodiac and the sequence of the signs from Taurus to Scorpius, and the two limiting signs are signified by the torch-bearers' attributes of bull's head and scorpion. Above Cautes and the bull's head is the Moon, and the Moon is the planet of the second and central decan of Taurus; above Cautopates and the scorpion is the Sun, and the Sun is the planet of the second and central decan of Scorpius; and between the Moon and the Sun stretch the other planets in the order of the days of the week, and it is in just that order that the planets fall in sequence to the second and central decans of the intervening signs:

←						
Sun	Saturn	Venus	Jupiter	Mercury	Mars	Moon
Scorpius	Libra	Virgo	Leo	Cancer	Gemini	Taurus
←						

Coincidence or design? Since the implications of the lay-out in the Bologna relief are potentially momentous, it would be as well to consider the alternatives — which are not a simple contrasted pair — most carefully. To start with that which would endow the monument with least significance, one might simply deny that the decanate was known to the Mysteries and attribute the apparent fit of the sequence of second decans to chance. To such a position it must be conceded first, as already emphasized, that there is nothing otherwise inexplicable in the lay-out of the Bologna relief that absolutely requires some hypothesis over and above the conceit of ordering the planets in the only sequence possible, i.e. that of the days of the week, between Luna in her usual place on the right and Sol in his usual place on the left; secondly, that the apparent use of the decans cannot be so readily demonstrated on any other monument of the cult and is certainly nowhere explicit in our various sources; thirdly, that the coincidence, though remarkable, is not so improbable as to rule mere chance quite out of the question. On this view, then, the fit with the sequence of second decans would be accidental and unconscious — a piquant accident perhaps, and one which might have appealed to a learned Mithraist if it had been pointed out to him, but in actuality only a piece of extraneous schematization imported by the present author.

A second view might admit the relevance of the decanate but confine its significance to the Bologna relief alone. The lay-out of the planets would then be the *jeu d'esprit* of a clever designer or learned Mithraist who realized not only that the planets could be set out in a readily recognizable order — that of the days of the week — between Luna and Sol in their given positions in the icon's upper corners, but also that that very sequence was the same as the order of a more arcane system — the decanate read in a certain way — which by happy chance intimated the signs or constellations of precisely that sector of the zodiac to which the icon alludes. The Bologna relief would, on this view, be unique because it expresses not an element of meaning which the cult at large read into the icon, but rather one man's learned elaboration or fantasy.

Now between the first and second alternatives the evidence offers little to choose — except for one detail. What hints at the decanate in the Bologna relief is the contrasted pair of secondary attributes next to the torchbearers on the margins, the bull's head and the scorpion, the one below the Moon on the right, the other below the Sun on the left. It is this pair that brings to the fore the zodiac and its signs, already implicit in the tauroctony, and which leads one to reflect whether there might not be a system which relates Taurus to the Moon, Scorpius to the Sun, and the intervening five planets to the intervening five signs in the given week-day order. In other words, without the bull's head and scorpion one would probably never consider the relevance of the decanate at all. Now the bull's head and scorpion are not common details in the tauroctonies; in fact they are very rare (see below). It was thus very much a matter of the individual designer's choice to go beyond the regular components of the scene and to include them on the Bologna relief. Should one suppose that the choice had nothing to do with the other striking — indeed unique — addition to the composition, namely the busts of the planets set above the scene between Luna and Sol, especially when the former seems to be the key to an explication of more profound meanings in the latter? Surely not. To accept one random piece of coincidence, that the week-day sequence on the Bologna relief happens by chance to fit the sequence of the second decans of the appropriate signs, is not unreasonable; to add a second coincidence, that the only monument to express that order just happens to be one of the very few to carry the symbols which can explain it, is to stretch plausibility beyond the breaking point. One must conclude, at the least, that the designer of the Bologna relief knew that his clever deployment of the planets in the week-day order carried with it, by means of the decanate, a set of correspondences with the signs of the zodiac implicated in the scene of the tauroctony.

There is, though, a third alternative: that the Bologna relief merely reveals and makes explicit what is already implicit in the composition of the standard icon. On this supposition, the primary fact would be that the scene of the tauroctony alludes to the arc of the zodiac containing the seven signs from Taurus in the west on the right to Scorpius in the east on the left. That fact is intimated in the composition not of course by the *inclusion* of Sol and Luna — they are present for other reasons — but by their *placement*: Luna on the right as the planetary deity of the central decan of Taurus, Sol on the left as the planetary deity of the central decan of Scorpius. The designer of the Bologna relief, on this hypothesis, has revealed the mystery by filling in the other five planets in their correct sequence as the decans of the intervening signs. We would be dealing, then, not merely with his private invention or elaboration but with an organic element within the body of the icon's meanings, an element consciously incorporated by the icon's inventors and accessible thereafter at least to the learned within the cult.

This last hypothesis is, I suggest, the correct one. Unlike the other two, it does not presuppose a fortunate coincidence in the lay-out of the Bologna relief. The planets are there deployed between Luna and Sol in the sequence of the central decans of the appropriate signs not by accident or because the decanate over that particular sector just happens to correspond with the required week-day sequence, but because Luna and Sol were *already* so located to right and left in the composition of the cult icon as to intimate the two flanking signs of Taurus and Scorpius. The designer of the Bologna relief merely filled in the gods of the central decans of the intervening signs, thus making explicit what was already implicit in the design of the standard tauroctony.

Crucial to our hypothesis is the fact that, though quite rare, the opposed symbols of the bull's head and scorpion are not unique to the Bologna relief. From that fact one may suppose that they give expression to some common meaning in the design of the icon in general rather than to some idiosyncrasy of a particular exemplar. The meaning assigned to the bull's head and scorpion is that Taurus and Scorpius are the flanking signs or constellations of the scene of the tauroctony. This is also one — but only one — of the several meanings of the pair of opposed torchbearers who regularly mark the margins of the scene and to whom the bull's head and scorpion belong as secondary attributes both on and apart from the tauroctony. But Luna and Sol are likewise a contrasted pair who, in the upper corners, regularly flank the scene. If, then, there is a relationship, such as we have postulated, between Luna and Sol on the one hand and Taurus and Scorpius, symbolized by the bull's head and scorpion or by the two torchbearers, on the other, it is likely to be a systematic one built into the icon's basic design.

Some support for our hypothesis is provided by those other reliefs of the tauroctony on which we find the bull's head and the scorpion. In the nature of the case, these are far too few to be decisive, but they do reinforce somewhat our postulated link between the luminaries and the signs.

Two other monuments show exactly the same arrangements as the Bologna relief. These are *CIMRM* 2006, a large and fine Dacian relief, and 335, the Ottaviano Zeno monument from Rome.[49] In each, not only is the bull's head on the side of Luna (right) and the scorpion on the side of Sol (left), but they are associated with the same torchbearers: the bull's head with Cautes (right) and

---

[49] To the Ottaviano Zeno monument we shall frequently return; the upper register with its row of seven altars and its gods is, together with the Bologna relief, one of the pivots of our discussion. For a long time, both the upper register and the main scene of the tauroctony were known only from drawings. Recently, however, the major part of the tauroctony came to light in São Paulo, Brasil. It was correctly identified by M. J. Vermaseren and published by him: *Mithriaca IV: Le monument d'Ottaviano Zeno et le culte de Mithra sur le Célius* (EPRO 16.4, Leiden 1978). The now extant parts of the monument confirm the general accuracy of the drawings of the whole.

the scorpion with Cautopates (left).[50] In a fourth monument, *CIMRM* 408 (an unusual relief from Rome),[51] we find a grazing ox instead of the bull's head. The symbols remain on their respective sides, the ox on the right below Luna and the scorpion on the left below Sol, but the torchbearers are in their alternative positions, Cautopates now appearing on the right and Cautes on the left.[52] This demonstrates that while the bull's head/ox and scorpion are attributes of the torchbearers, each is not invariably the attribute of the *same* torchbearer.[53] Location on a particular side appears to be more fundamental.

[50] Some peculiarities of the Ottaviano Zeno relief must be mentioned. Sol and Luna are on the upper register, not part of the main scene. The torchbearers are (uniquely) represented by their torches alone, respectively upright and inverted, leaning against trees, with the secondary attributes alongside. The set of symbols on the right is found on the recovered part of the tauroctony, which seems to confirm the set on the left. In the photographs of the recovered tauroctony the animal's head appears more like a goat's than a bull's. Vermaseren ([above, n. 49], 19) initially so reports it, but subsequently (20-21, 36 ff.) speaks of it as a bull's; he reports (addendum to p. 19) that the curator at São Paulo later confirmed to him "que la tête du chevreau serait plutôt celle d'un veau." Given the other instances, the benefit of the doubt should probably incline to the bovine rather than the caprine. See, however, n. 42 (above) on the somewhat leonine appearance of the bull's head on the Bologna relief. The reliefs of the torchbearers which are shown in the drawings one above the other on the left and which were recovered on an earlier occasion (also by Vermaseren — see the *CIMRM* description [335]) do not belong to the original relief. Vermaseren's conjecture (p. 23) that they come from the side-benches of the same mithraeum seems to me likely to be correct.

[51] For a photograph, see Vermaseren (above, n. 49), Pl. 28. In general, these monuments with the bull and scorpion seem to be especially rich — or "garrulous" (Richard Gordon's evocative term) — in their symbolism. 408 has, in addition, a Pegasus and *two* birds (one the customary raven) by Sol and a snake by Luna. 2006 has a small lion's head (overlooked in the descriptions) on the cave's rocky border below Sol.

[52] Generally, it is more usual for Cautes to be on the left and Cautopates on the right on Italian monuments and very much more usual for Cautes to be on the right and Cautopates on the left on those of the Rhine and Danube provinces. Statistics in J. R. Hinnells, "The Iconography of Cautes and Cautopates, I: The Data," *JMS* 1 (1976), 36-67, fig. 3. The logic behind these alternatives I have explained as follows (*art. cit.* [above, n. 37], 8 ff. — to my knowledge, there is no alternative explanation in the field). The tauroctony is celestially aligned: east is to the left, west to the right. Cautes with his raised torch on the left symbolizes the Sun rising in the east; Cautopates with his lowered torch on the right symbolizes the Sun setting in the west. But Cautes and Cautopates also represent the signs of Taurus and Scorpius. In Taurus the Sun is climbing from the spring equinox towards the summer solstice, hence Cautes' raised torch; in Scorpius the Sun is descending again from the autumn equinox towards the winter solstice, hence Cautopates' lowered torch. But, as we have seen, in the stellar scheme of the tauroctony Taurus belongs in the west on the right and Scorpius in the east on the left. Hence the other pattern of composition with Cautes on the right and Cautopates on the left.

I might add that in my article (6 ff.) I proposed a yet more intimate identification of the torchbearers with the two bright, red stars Aldebaran, the lucida of Taurus, and Antares, the lucida of Scorpius. These stars occupied, according to some ancient sources, the exact centre (i.e. the 15th degree) of their signs. This refinement, if correct, would add some weight to our argument concerning the luminaries (and other planets) and the *central* decans of the signs.

[53] Generally, Cautes has the bull's head, Cautopates the scorpion. But, in addition to 408, we find Cautopates with a recumbent bull in 694, an unusual relief of that torchbearer alone surrounded by various other symbols as well as the bull: a lunar crescent (N.B.!), an upturned jar with water flowing from it, reeds, and a rocky background. (There is no extant corresponding relief of Cautes.) It is interesting that in these two instances where Cautopates is associated with

But even that correlation can be broken; for in the fifth and last example, *CIMRM* 2306 (Moesian, from Tirguşor near Constanţa), we find the scorpion on the *right* — with Cautopates again. (On the left, instead of the bull's head, Cautes has as secondary attributes a pine cone and a column against which he leans.) Significantly, however, 2306 is also one of those few monuments on which Sol and Luna have exchanged places:[54] Sol is here in the upper right, Luna in the upper left. So the scorpion on the right is beneath Sol on the right. In sum, the one relationship to remain constant across the monuments is that between the attributes and the luminaries.[55] Of course, the sample is tiny and

---

an ox or bull, it is with the whole animal, not the head alone. Of Cautes with a scorpion there is likewise a single instance in addition to 408. It too is a separate representation of the one torch-bearer: *CIMRM* 124, a statue from Rusicade in Numidia. Cautes has at his feet a scorpion, and also a lion (cf. n. 51, above, on the small lion's head between Sol and Cautopates with his scorpion on 2006). The companion piece with Cautopates is here extant (*CIMRM* 123), but the attributes are a dolphin and a bird.

[54] See above, n. 39.

[55] I have excluded three monuments that figure in Vermaseren's analysis ([above, n. 49], 37 ff.). (1) *CIMRM* 1973: Vermaseren (p. 40) is rightly tentative about this relief from Apulum, but considers it possible that Cautes (r.) may be holding a bull's head and Cautopates (l.) a scorpion. That is possible for Cautes, though his object is now no more than a shapeless mass. Of Cautopates I would say from autopsy that it is very doubtful whether he is carrying anything at all (other than his torch). However, if Cautes and Cautopates are in fact carrying a bull's head and a scorpion respectively, the monument would be precisely analogous to 693 (the Bologna relief) and 2006 in the positioning of the torchbearers, their secondary attributes, and the luminaries. On the row of seven altars and other symbols above the bull-killing on this relief, see above, n. 27. (2) and (3) the seal gem stones 2354-55: The scorpions here are, I believe, simply the creatures that are regularly found at the bull's genitals in tauroctonies, somewhat displaced (towards Cautes) because they would otherwise be lost in the tiny scale of the composition. On the same side of the composition, near Cautes, is a palm branch "auquel une tête semble être attachée" (Vermaseren, p. 38). The palm branch is below Sol and is a known solar symbol. That being so, I would read the head (if such it is) as a lion's, the lion being another notable solar symbol. If it is a bull's head, then it would be an exception to my hypothesis on the exclusive linking of the bull's head to Luna and the scorpion to Sol. Even so, however, I would argue that the gem stones, being in the first place *private* articles and in the second somewhat chaotic in their plethora of symbols, are unreliable guides to any principle of composition in the icon in general. To add to the confusion, the symbols here are both on the *same* side of the composition.

CIMRM 2354 and 2355 are important items in R. Merkelbach's case that symbols of the grades and their planetary gods are also found in the tauroctony (*Mithras* [above, n. 4], 82, 393 [Abb. 165, 166]). Certainly there is a wealth of subsidiary symbols in these two gems, many of which can indeed be related to the grades. However, only by straining the evidence can complete *sets* of grade or planetary symbols be deciphered. For example, to account for the Nymphus/Venus and to obviate apparent duplication for the Leo/Jupiter (to which a thunderbolt is obviously to be assigned), Merkelbach must read as a dove a bird which is manifestly an eagle. Of the details which concern us here, Merkelbach reads the scorpion as a tortoise (Mercury/Raven), and the lion's head against the palm branch he ignores (yet another Leo symbol?).

Not in Vermaseren's analysis, but relevant to our case, is *CIMRM* 2252, a relief from Oescus in Moesia. The *CIMRM* description has Cautes holding "a [second] torch or double-axe downwards with his l. h." From inspection I can confirm, however, that the object is actually an animal's head, and though it perhaps looks more like a sheep's I would be inclined to take it as a bull's. Cautes is on the right, so the bull's head (if that is what it is) is on the lunar side — but not below Luna, for the luminaries were not included on this monument. (Cautopates on the other side has no scorpion or anything that could be seen as such. He is definitely not, as *CIMRM* thinks possi-

can establish nothing conclusively. But it does suggest that it is a given of the design that the bull's head and the scorpion, when they figure in the composition, are related respectively to Luna and Sol. The exceptional relief, 2306, shows that when the luminaries shift sides, so do those attributes of the torchbearers — or at least so does the scorpion.[56] One surmises that behind that datum was a perceived link between the luminaries and the zodiacal signs intimated by the pair of symbols. And the only shared link between the Moon and Taurus, on the one hand, and the Sun and Scorpius, on the other, is that the two planets are the presiding gods of the central decans of the respective signs.

Let us allow, then, at least provisionally and hypothetically, that the Bologna relief reveals a hidden element in the general design of the tauroctony: that Sol and Luna are so positioned as to intimate through the decanate the final terms of both a planetary and a zodiacal sequence. The planets, then, are as implicated in whatever it is that the tauroctony portrays as are the signs. The presence of the signs in the scene is the more obvious, since so many — in fact virtually all — of its components allude to them, either directly or through the paranatellonta. The presence of the planets is a more arcane matter; for it must be deduced indirectly from the signs, its key is an unstated piece of technical astrology, and except in the Bologna relief it is conveyed only by the disposition of Sol and Luna and occasionally by that of a pair of secondary attributes of the torchbearers.

What purpose was served by incorporating the planets as well as the signs in the scene of the bull-killing in so precise, learned, and yet cryptic a manner? Here one can as yet only add conjecture to conjecture, but at least the outline of an answer should be hazarded. The tauroctony depicts a great act of salvation — few, I think, would quarrel with that premise. To realize that salvation for the initiate a process and a route are needed. That process and route are defined in one form in the grade structure of the cult, and they involve, as we now know, a passage under the tutelary powers of the planets in a certain

---

ble, touching the bull's tail. There is an object in his lifted left hand and I argue [*Apulum* 22 (1985), 56 f.] that it is a second torch. Whether a figure who carries a raised torch as well as a lowered can still be called "Cautopates" is an intriguing problem which presents itself in the context of certain other monuments too and which I also address [*ibid.*].)

[56] That 2306 has been *systematically* inverted is suggested by the exchange of position not only of the luminaries but also of the torchbearers. Cautes is on the left, Cautopates on the right. This, as already noted (above, n. 52), contravenes the norm for the European frontier provinces. But that norm seems to be especially well observed in Moesia. Hinnells ([above, n. 52], 64) notes no exceptions among the 16 tauroctonies which he lists for Moesia Superior and only two (one queried) among the 16 for Moesia Inferior. Those two in the lower province are 2292 where the torchbearers are in fact in their normal positions and out present relief, 2306. (See, though, my *Apulum* article [above, n. 55], 45 ff., for certain further complications in these statistics and those for Dacia.) Thus, in 2306 we see further evidence of a systematic inversion of "left" and "right," "east" and "west."

unusual and evocative order. This is in some sense — again, we do not know precisely how — a celestial journey. But the heavens, we know, are incorporated in the icon which expresses the central salvific event, overtly as a precise arrangement of constellation symbols defining a particular tract of the heavens. Here, then, is another "map" of the *via salutis*.[57] But is it related to the "map" of the grade structure? Is the journey among the constellations and the signs part of the journey among the planets and vice versa, or are the two quite separate — consecutive perhaps, or entirely unrelated? The Mysteries, it seems, saw the two as intimately bound together, and to express that union they selected one of the astrological modes of relating the planets to the signs of the zodiac, namely the decanate, and built it into the icon's design. The chosen relationship does not yield the same planetary order within the icon as in the grade structure — since the grade order is unique, that would have been impossible. But it does yield a sequence consonant with what we saw to be one of the grade order's underlying principles, the blending of the spatial with the temporal. For the decanate is based on the distribution of the planets sequentially to thirds of signs by order of distance, yet in the selection of the same decan of successive signs it yields, as we have also seen, the weekday order. The road of salvation is a journey through and from both cosmic dimensions of space and time; this truth is as nicely reflected in the incorporation of the planets in the tauroctony as it is in their ordering in the grade sequence.

The decanate, as we know, is a mode of relating the planets to the constellations and the signs. Now ever since Plato and the *Timaeus* it was a commonplace of natural philosophy that the planetary world and the stellar world are fundamentally different. Although for Plato the distinction was essentially one of plurality or variety ("the Different") *versus* unity ("the Same"), it was generally seen as an opposition between two directions of motion.[58] The stars move westwards with the motion of the universe itself, the planets —

---

[57] The tauroctony as celestial map will be the subject of another study, covering what might be called the road of the signs and constellations, as the present study covers the road — or roads — of the planets. It will include a full and proper treatment of the stellar components of the tauroctony, an analysis of the zodiacs on Mithraic monuments, and, of course, consideration of the important testimony of Porphyry (*De antro* 21-28) on the gates of genesis and apogenesis in Cancer and Capricorn. These, together with the various planetary matters of the present study, really form a single complex, interlocking whole. Their exclusion, by and large, from the present study is thus somewhat artificial, but at the present early stage of our explorations it is inevitable. There are many routes into the Mysteries; the road of the planets will serve well enough for now.

[58] *Timaeus* 36C-D: the creator-god "named the movement of the outer circle after the nature of the Same, of the inner after the nature of the Different. The circle of the Same he caused to revolve from left to right, and the circle of the Different from right to left on an axis inclined to it; and made the master revolution that of the Same. For he left the circle of the Same whole and undivided, but slit the inner circle six times to make seven unequal circles ..." (trans. D. Lee). Cf. the (earlier) simile of the Spindle of Necessity in the *Republic* (616-617), where the inner rings of the spindle's whorl revolve in the opposite direction to the outermost.

though they also partake of the universal motion — eastwards. The Mithraists, we happen to know, were interested in that fundamental opposition. We know too that for them salvation (if we may so call the flight and passage of the soul) was somehow implicated in the two motions. The evidence is Origen quoting Celsus on the *symbolon* of the ladder (*Contra Celsum* 6.22): "in it (sc. the *teletē* of Mithras) there is a *symbolon* of the two celestial revolutions (τῶν δύο τῶν ἐν οὐρανῷ περιόδων), that of the fixed stars and that assigned to the planets, and of the passage (διεξόδου) of the soul through them." We shall return to this important testimony towards the end of our study, but it is worth introducing here to demonstrate that the relationship between the planetary world and the stellar world definitely figures in Mithraic doctrine. That relationship, I suggest, is also explored in the composition of the cult's icon, where the two worlds are reconciled — in a very "scientific" fashion — through the astrological system of the decanate.

If the order of the planets as we find it on the Bologna relief is, as I contend, "built into" the composition of the icon of the tauroctony, then it is arguable that the relatively common motif of a row of seven altars,[59] when it appears in the same location, i.e. extended across the top of the bull-killing between Luna and Sol, intimates the planets in that order and with the same connotations of the presiding deities of the second decans of the signs "within the scene," namely those from Taurus to Scorpius. That would be the altars' primary significance, at least for those with knowledge of the arcana of the composition. But being, as it were, blanks, they could also imply various other orders, including the grade order, much as can the seven vacant arches on the pavements of the Sette Sfere and Sette Porte mithraea in Ostia (above, p. 14). The motif of the seven altars above the scene is particularly a feature of Danubian tauroctonies, but it also occurs in Italy. On the important Ottaviano Zeno monument (*CIMRM* 335) and the Barberini fresco (390) the altars' concomitants allow considerable further explication. It will be the starting point of our discussion of those monuments (below) that there is an implied planetary order, that of the Bologna relief, in their sets of altars.

A final detail of the Bologna relief requires comment. The central bust in the row of planetary gods is of course that of Jupiter. Its centrality is emphasized first by the placement of the head of the bull-killing Mithras directly below it, and secondly by the angles of the busts themselves; for while the heads of the other gods are more or less in profile and face inwards towards Jupiter, that of Jupiter himself is full-face and looks directly outwards from the relief at the viewer.[60] It seems, then, that there is more to Jupiter's position

---

[59] See above, p. 12 with n. 27, on sets of seven in the icon.

[60] The poses of the other gods facing inwards towards Jupiter replicate those of Cautes and Cautopates underneath facing inwards towards Mithras. It is worth noting that in Luna's case the pose overrides the usual convention in Mithraic iconography that has her facing outwards and

than the luck of falling in the middle of the sequence that begins with the Moon and ends with the Sun. Jupiter in that position is uniquely privileged and the designer has definitely emphasized that fact.

Why? One answer would relate to public religion. Jupiter, after all, is the supreme god of the traditional Roman system. The designer, then, has exploited the accident of his setting in the middle of the given sequence to honour his primacy.

There may, however, be other more esoteric reasons. First, it is at this central point, and at this point alone, that the order of the Bologna relief (1) coincides with the cult's grade order (2):

(1)	Sun	Saturn	Venus	*Jupiter*	Mercury	Mars	Moon
(2)	Saturn	Sun	Moon	*Jupiter*	Mars	Venus	Mercury

The emphasis on Jupiter in the expressed sequence would thus serve to prompt a recollection of that other most germane of orders in which Jupiter also stands at the centre, and would incidentally acknowledge the centrality of the grade over which Jupiter presides, the Lions who are the first true "participants" (μετέχοντες) of the Mysteries.[61]

The mention of the Lions introduces yet another factor. It is at this point that the grade order and the order of second-decan gods impinge particularly closely on each other. For the Lion, as well as Jupiter, is in the centre of each sequence. Jupiter, as we have seen, is not only the tutelary god of the Lion grade but also the presiding god of the central decan of Leo, the Lion sign. In each of these two modes Jupiter thus intimates the leonine.

A further tie linking Jupiter, Leo and the Lions is that it is not only the Mithraic Lions who are literally *tutela Iovis* but also the sign of Leo itself. For in the Roman calendric system (ultimately derived from Greek sources) which assigned the twelve gods — in effect, the Olympians — to the twelve signs or months, Leo fell to Jupiter. In that system *tutela* was used as the technical term,[62] and it was perhaps from that source that the Mysteries drew the terminology for relating grades to planets as we find it in the Sa. Prisca dipinti. It is with Jupiter and the Lions — and there only — that the exoteric system coincides with the esoteric, both Leo and the Leones being *tutela Iovis*.

---

away (i.e. to the right) when Sol is facing inwards, or full-face when Sol is posed in the same way. (Even if the fragment in the centre of the upper rim is a restoration, the poses of all seven deities can be inferred from those whose originality is not in question: see Appendix.)

[61] Porphyry *De abstinentia* 4.16. On the place of the Lions in the structure of the grade hierarchy, see esp. Gordon (above, n. 4), 32 f.

[62] E.g. Manilius 2.434 *noscere* tutelas *adiectaque numina signis*. For the system, see *ibid.* 433-447; F. Cumont, "Zodiacus," *Dictionnaire des antiquités* (Daremberg-Saglio), 5.1055 f.; Bouché-Leclercq (above, n. 7), 183 f.

Two other monuments now take on a particular relevance. The first is *CIMRM* 2198, a Danubian relief whose exact find-spot is unknown. On it is a lion's mask set at the summit above Mithras' head and forming with the busts of Sol on the left and Luna on the right an unmistakable trio.[63] That trio intimates, by the explicit inclusion of the middle term, the planetary order of the Bologna relief — and, I would argue, of the icon in general:

CIMRM 2198:	Sol	-------------------	Lion	--------------------	Luna
Bologna relief:	Sun	Saturn	Venus	Jupiter	Mercury	Mars	Moon

The second monument is the Barberini fresco (390; and see diagram below, fig. 5, p. 91). As already noted, the Barberini fresco is one of those monuments which have a row of altars extending between Luna and Sol. But in the Barberini fresco there are only *six* altars. However, in the centre, and precisely where one would look for the seventh, is a lion's head. But this lion's head is not a self-contained object like the mask in 2198. Rather, it is the head of a figure which is represented in full, namely, that lion-headed, snake-encircled god who plays such an enigmatic role in the cult's theology. We shall return to him later; for the present, the point is that the leonine head, as M. J. Vermaseren observes,[64] hides a seventh and central altar; alternatively, one may suppose that the leonine head substitutes for, or in a sense *is*, the seventh altar. Again, Jupiter is evoked through his association with the Lion grade and with Leo, and the planetary order of the Bologna relief is thus intimated for the row of altars.

We have still to mention the most remarkable feature of the Jupiter of the Bologna relief. To put it sharply and paradoxically — as it should be put — he is not Jupiter at all. He is distinguished by none of the attributes of Jupiter. Instead, he wears the attribute of another god altogether: the *kalathos* or *modius* of Serapis set on his head. And yet, of course, by position in the planetary sequence he must be, and is, Jupiter. It seems, then, that the designer has been at pains to present a Jupiter who both is and is not Jupiter, a Jupiter who here in this setting is not himself but Serapis.[65]

---

[63] *CIMRM* incorrectly reports Sol on the right and Luna on the left.

[64] *Mithriaca III: The Mithraeum at Marino* (EPRO 16.3, Leiden 1982), 13. Professor Ugo Bianchi tells me that he doubts that the figure on the Barberini fresco is lion-headed at all. If that is so, then my argument is complicated rather than invalidated. For the figure is certainly snake-encircled, and from that and its pose one can tell that it is clearly a representation of this type of deity, one of whose principal iconographic features is the lion's head and who is known, conventionally and when a neutral term is needed, as the "lion-headed" god (*vel. sim.*). The lion's head is thus intimated, if not expressed. But I believe that in fact it is lion-headed: see Pl. 16 in Vermaseren (above). Professor Vermaseren confirmed to me his belief, from his first autopsy, that the figure is lion-headed.

[65] I am here assuming that the designer is that of the original relief, not a restorer. The case for the authenticity of the fragment in the centre of the upper rim and thus for the integrity of the

What purpose or meaning underlies this striking paradox one cannot precisely tell. Presumably an equation of sorts is intended, an equation such as one finds in the inscription of the *cippus* from the Mithraeum of the Baths of Caracalla (*CIMRM* 463). There Zeus is equated not only with Serapis but also with Helios and Mithras too.[66]

That Serapis played some part in Mithraic theology is attested by the heads of the god discovered in mithraea in Rome (Sa. Prisca, *CIMRM* 479), Merida (783), and London (818, the finest example). Unfortunately, the original placement of these monuments in relation to other material within their mithraea is unknown, so that little can be deduced from them.[67] Much more revealing is the bust set in the larger and upper of the two tauroctonies of the Dura Mithraeum (*CIMRM* 40). Serapis, with *kalathos/modius* and, in addition, solar rays, is positioned at the summit of the arch which frames the composition and which is here adorned with a zodiac, in precisely the same place as the Jupiter-Serapis of the Bologna relief, the lion's head of 2198, and the lion-headed god of the Barberini fresco.[68] And here at Dura he is even more obviously the central figure of a trio with Sol and Luna, for the luminaries

---

whole relief is set out in the Appendix. The case depends, indeed, largely on arguments that no restorer would or could have known the appropriateness of the presentation of Jupiter as Serapis (or Serapis in place of Jupiter). If the fragment's authenticity is not accepted, these pages (32-34) are to be discounted.

[66] The monument was probably "recycled," Μίτρας (*sic*) on the front being recut over Σάραπις (see Moretti *IGUR* no. 194). Perhaps the mithraeum itself had originally been a Serapeum.

[67] A. N. Oikonomides has suggested that the London Serapis head formed part of a huge "acrolith" group, taken apart for safekeeping, in which it would have occupied the same place in the composition as the Bologna Jupiter-Serapis: *Mithraic Art* (Chicago 1975), 9-22. Among this group of finds was a female head, thought to be Minerva's, but which Oikonomides identifes as that of an Artemis-Luna. But the pose of the head, angled to the right and slightly raised, is wrong for a Luna in her proper place on the right of the composition. The pose would suit a Venus set among the gods on the left in a planetary sequence as on the Bologna relief — Oikonomides believes that there was originally such a set in the London composition — but the severe expression and features of the head tell against such a supposition.

The Sa. Prisca Serapis head, which is made of stucco, was discovered with two others, also of stucco, one female and the other (a fragment) male. Vermaseren and Van Essen ([above, n. 2], 134-136) acknowledge that these other two could be Sol and Luna and could have been attached to the outer face of the border of the cult-niche. For the Serapis head there was apparently insufficient space below the ceiling at the summit of the border, but Vermaseren and Van Essen allow that it could have been attached within the niche itself, perhaps above the bull's head where there are nail holes. Thus, there could at Santa Prisca have been a trio of (l. to r.) Sol-Serapis-Luna. (The heads are assumed to have come from the cult-niche area although they were discovered a short distance away, in Room W'.)

[68] A lion-headed god was perhaps also in the same place in the large cult-relief from Mithraeum II at Poetovio (*CIMRM* 1510). The relevant fragment is lost, and the detail is known only from a drawing: reproduced in H. von Gall, "The Lion-Headed and the Human-Headed God in the Mithraic Mysteries," *Etudes mithriaques* (Acta Iranica 17, Leiden 1978), 511-525, Pl. 31, fig. 9. A link between the lion-headed god and Serapis might be provided by *CIMRM* 611, a statue of the former with *kalathos*. But the monument is known only from a drawing, and there are serious doubts about its genuineness.

were set close in beside him.[69] We find, then, a *complex* which is defined first by *position* within the icon and secondly by *relationship* as the middle term between two others:

Bologna:	Sun	Jupiter as Serapis	Moon
2198:	Sol	lion's head	Luna
Barberini:	Sol	lion-headed god	Luna
Dura:	Luna	Serapis, with solar rays	Sol

I postpone exploring the ramifications of this complex until the introduction of our final major monument, namely the upper register of the Ottaviano Zeno group (*CIMRM* 335), in a later section.

VI

The credibility of our analysis of the Bologna relief in terms of the decanate will be much enhanced if it can be shown that elsewhere too Mithraism made use of the astrological schemes for relating the planets and the signs of the zodiac. This can indeed be done, not with the decanate, admittedly, but with the systems of planetary "houses" (οἶκοι) and "exaltations" (ὑφώματα).[70] Thus, for example, the circle of the zodiac surrounding the Sidon tauroctony (*CIMRM* 75) is so positioned that Aries, the exaltation of the Sun, is shown leaping up at the bust of Sol and Taurus, the exaltation of the Moon, leaping up at the bust of Luna. The design makes the juxtapositions and their intention unmistakable. We find the same association of luminaries and animals, apart from a zodiac, in the Mauls relief (1400): a small ram next to the bust of Sol, a small bull next to Luna.[71] Again, with the ring zodiacs of the London (810) and Siscia (1472) reliefs, Taurus is set next to Luna and Leo, the house of the Sun, next to Sol.[72] At a more fundamental level, and as a matter of doc-

---

[69] The luminaries were in the unusual reversed position (see above, n. 39), as were their symbols in the smaller and lower relief (*CIMRM* 37). At some stage, and for some unknown reason, they were removed, but the remains of Sol's rays attest their original setting.

[70] On these systems see Bouché-Leclercq (above, n. 7), 182-199. Note that the "houses" of ancient astrology are entirely different from the "houses" of modern astrology. The latter correspond to what the ancients called "places" (*loci*).

[71] The composition is asymmetric in that both animals are shown running from right to left (perhaps signifying the proper motion of the luminaries from west to east: see above, n. 37). On the Sidon relief, incidentally, Sol and Luna are in reversed positions.

[72] Note, in 810, the juxtapositioning of Taurus and the bulls of Luna's *biga*; in both reliefs, of Taurus and the head of the bull killed by Mithras.

trine, we know that the Mysteries used the system of houses to validate their cosmological setting of Mithras "at the equinoxes." [73]

For more detailed consideration, however, I select a monument on which an astrological scheme for relating signs and planets is more fully exploited than on those mentioned above. This is the representation of the birth of Mithras from Housesteads on Hadrian's Wall (*CIMRM* 860). The scene is surrounded by a zodiac, arranged — it is my contention — according to the system of planetary houses. Thus, the composition is in a sense the reverse of the Bologna relief. The latter, we saw, intimated the signs through the planets; the former, it will be demonstrated, intimates the planets through the signs. In both, one set is explicit, the other implicit: in one, the planets "contain" the signs; in the other, the signs "contain" the planets.

In the Housesteads birth scene Mithras emerges not from the usual rock but from the split shell of an egg; half of the shell is below and serves in lieu of the "rock," the other half is on top of Mithras' head. [74] Otherwise the iconography is normal: Mithras is shown from the waist up, naked, and carries a sword in his right hand and a torch in his left. The zodiac is set in relief on an ovoid frame which, at its inner rim, replicates the egg from which Mithras is born — but in reverse: the broad end of the ovoid is at the top, whereas the broad end of the actual birth egg is at the bottom. [75]

The frame that carries the zodiac is interrupted at the bottom by the monument's base, except for its inner rim which is complete and tangent to the base's top (see diagram, fig. 2). Thus, the frame can also be seen as a horseshoe in shape. This is important, since instead of an unbroken ring of signs we find a sequence which has a definite starting point and a definite end. The signs start, in fact, with Aquarius at the lower left and run clockwise up, around, and down to Capricorn at the lower right. [76]

---

[73] Porphyry *De antro nympharum* 24. Porphyry's argument is deficient in logic and the Greek text is demonstrably corrupt: see my "The Seat of Mithras at the Equinoxes," *JMS* 1 (1976), 95-98, with an emendation to solve both problems. However, that Porphyry's argument somehow depends on the system of houses is obvious and not in dispute. It could of course be objected that the argument is not that of the Mysteries at all but rather a learned rationalization of Porphyry and his sources. Such an argument is suggested by R. Turcan when he speaks of the "argumentation astrologique" as "bien caractéristique de Numénius" (*Mithras Platonicus* [EPRO 47, Leiden 1975], 77). I find it, though, equally characteristic of the Mysteries, and I do not see on what criteria either source can be excluded.

[74] It is thus somewhat paradoxical to call the scene a "rock-birth," though that of course is what it is. For the split egg shell the obvious parallel is the Phanes of the Modena relief (*CIMRM* 695), a work probably recycled into Mithraic use because of its analogies with the Mysteries' lion-headed god.

[75] Within the ovoid the stone has been entirely cut away except for the figure of Mithras and the two halves of the shell. This has the effect first of emphasizing the egg-like shape of the frame and secondly, since Mithras' hands are set against the inner rim, of suggesting that Mithras bears aloft the sign-studded vault of heaven.

[76] It is a peculiarity of the Housesteads zodiac that Aquarius as well as Capricorn is represented as a fish-tailed creature. In part, this is probably a mere matter of balancing the composition,

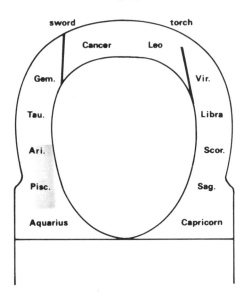

Fig. 2 *Composition of the zodiac of the Housesteads birth scene (CIMRM* 860: from a tracing of the silhouette).

It is this commencement with Aquarius that reveals a special intention behind the composition of the zodiac on the Housesteads birth scene. Had the designer wished to add a zodiac merely to give a certain cosmic significance to the scene, he would almost certainly have begun the sequence in the usual way with one of the tropic or equinoctial signs.[77] The fact that he did not do so suggests that his arrangement was purposeful. What, then, might the under-lying logic be?

Now the Housesteads rock-birth is a highly symmetrical composition. It is balanced left against right, and the strong central vertical of Mithras' trunk and head emphasizes the fact. The signs thus divide into two hexads:

---

though it is a pleasing and innovative touch that reveals a degree of imagination in the designer. But in emphasizing "fishiness" and the sea, the designer is also, I believe, at pains to signal the element of water at the base of the universe. In contrast, fire is signalled by the pair at the top, Cancer, the sign of the summer solstice, and Leo, the house of the Sun.

[77] The norm may easily be verified in H. G. Gundel's catalogue of surviving ancient zodiacs: "Zodiakos," *RE* 10 A (Munich 1972), 461-710, at 611-694. A similar norm applies to ring zodiacs (i.e. those without an identifiable starting point to the sequence of signs): with very few excep-tions, the cardinal points (i.e. 12, 3, 6 and 9 o'clock) are occupied either by the tropic and equinoctial signs or by the tropic and equinoctial points (i.e. the boundaries between Pisces and Aries, Gemini and Cancer, Virgo and Libra, and Sagittarius and Capricorn). I shall be treating of these matters and their application in Mithraic zodiacs at some length in another study.

left	*right*
Cancer	Leo
Gemini	Virgo
Taurus	Libra
Aries	Scorpius
Pisces	Sagittarius
Aquarius	Capricorn

But there is a second division within the zodiac which is physically marked, unlike the first which was a matter of composition only. Also, this second division is asymmetric in that it separates an unequal number of signs on either side. The division is that effected by Mithras' sword and torch which obtrude into the zodiac frame: above are the two signs of Cancer and Leo, below are the remaining ten. In combination, these two divisions yield the following structure:

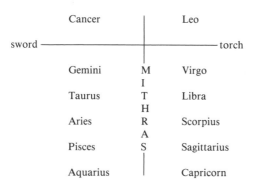

But this composition, thus analysed, is not unique to the Mysteries. Rather, it is another example of an adaptation to their esoteric world of a structure from a different and more public discipline. Essentially, it is the structure of the planetary houses,[78] and I do not doubt that any viewer familiar with astrology (even in a superficial way) would have recognized it as such:

---

[78] The same structure, I have argued, underlies the composition of the zodiac of the Ponza Mithraeum: see my "Interpreting the Ponza Zodiac: I," *JMS* 1 (1976), 1-19, at 6 f.

	lunar	*solar*	
Cancer	Moon	Sun	Leo
Gemini	Mercury	Mercury	Virgo
Taurus	Venus	Venus	Libra
Aries	Mars	Mars	Scorpius
Pisces	Jupiter	Jupiter	Sagittarius
Aquarius	Saturn	Saturn	Capricorn

The system of houses divides the zodiac into two halves, the "solar semi-circle" consisting of the signs from Leo to Capricorn and the "lunar semi-circle" consisting of those from Cancer to Aquarius.[79] In the lunar semicircle, one notes, the signs are ordered in reverse, so that on the Housesteads monument, in so far as it exemplifies the system, the zodiac is to be "read" downwards on each side (see diagram, above) rather than clockwise in a circle as we did initially. The two semicircles are headed by the houses of the Sun and the Moon themselves, Leo and Cancer. The luminaries have only one house each, but the other five planets have two, a "diurnal" house on the solar side and a "nocturnal" on the lunar. The signs are allotted in pairs in the order of the planets' distances from Earth (i.e. in the "Chaldean" order). Thus, Mercury has Virgo and Gemini, the pair next to the houses of the luminaries. The following pair, Libra and Taurus, falls to Venus, and the next, Scorpius and Aries, to Mars. Jupiter has Sagittarius and Pisces, and Saturn the final pair, Capricorn and Aquarius.

The Housesteads rock-birth thus reveals — or conceals, it could equally well be said — through its disposition of the signs in a pattern suggestive of the houses, the planets "within" the signs. The planetary arrangement is a singularly neat one: the order descends — or ascends — symmetrically on each side through balanced pairs, except at the summit above the division formed by Mithras' implements where the luminaries together preside over their respective sets. The placing of "Sun" and "Moon" opposite each other at the top of the monument is particularly appropriate, since that of course is where we find them in the Mysteries' principal icon. The Housesteads rock-birth thus conveys, through its system of inner equivalents, resonances of the

---

[79] The terms ἡμικύκλιον ἡλιακόν/σεληνιακόν are Ptolemy's: *Tetrabiblos* 1.17.

tauroctony.[80] The placing of "Saturn," too, in the guise of Capricorn and Aquarius, may be significant, though the links are more tenuous. At the bottom of the composition, it recalls the setting of the vast Saturn-Oceanus at the base of the tauroctony of the Sa. Prisca Mithraeum and of the related reclining figure, snake-encircled, at the bottom right of complex Danubian tauroctonies.[81]

But the principal reason why the arrangement of the zodiac by planetary houses is so appropriate, and hence perhaps the determining factor in its choice for the composition of the monument, is that it intimates the *thema mundi*, the nativity of the universe. For it was in their houses, according to certain astrologers, that the planets were first set when the world was created.[82] It is right, then, that an arrangement which signals the birth of the world should adorn a monument which celebrates the birth of its ruling power.

Above Mithras' head, at the apex of the monument, is the boundary between Cancer and Leo. This, as we saw, is an unusual point to place at the summit of a zodiac, and its oddity led us to a realization of the principle of balance at work in the composition: it is a point of division between the lunar houses and the solar houses, the other point being the Capricorn-Aquarius boundary marked by the split of the zodiac at the base of the monument. But the Cancer-Leo boundary is also a place of significance in its own right, and thus independently a fitting point to occupy the summit of the composition.

Before looking at the astrological connotations of the Cancer-Leo boundary, however, we should introduce another monument. A second monument will sometimes bring into sharper focus a detail on a first, suggesting significance in the composition that might otherwise be passed over.

There are extant two representations of the Mithraic rock-birth which also carry zodiacs. The first is the Housesteads monument, the second a relief from Trier (*CIMRM* 985). As on the Housesteads monument, the zodiac on the Trier relief surrounds the nascent Mithras, except at the bottom where rocks obtrude into the ring of signs. Unusually — indeed, uniquely among Mithraic zodiacs — only half of the signs are represented. But the choice follows the most normal division of the zodiac by tropics and equinoxes.

---

[80] Note, however, that the positions are reversed, for Cancer (= Luna) is on the left, Leo (= Sol) on the right.

[81] On Saturn-Oceanus see M. J. Vermaseren, "The Miraculous Birth of Mithras," *Mnemosyne*, Ser. 4, 4 (1951 = *Studia van Hoorn*), 285-301, at 292-294. Note also *CIMRM* 1127, a rock-birth from Heddernheim, Mithraeum III: the stone is carved on three sides, the birth scene being on the front; on the right side, below Cautopates, is a reclining Oceanus identified as such in the inscription (the corresponding area on the other side is occupied by symbols of *Celum* [*sic*] — eagle, thunderbolt, and star-studded globe with crossed zones).

[82] The five planets proper were set in their solar houses. On the *thema mundi* see Firmicus Maternus *Math.* 3.1, Macrobius *In somn.* 1.21.23-27, Bouché-Leclercq (above, n. 7), 185 f.

Chosen are the six northern or summer signs (i.e. those north of the equator traversed by the Sun in spring and summer). The sequence starts with Aries, the sign of the spring equinox, at the lower left and runs clockwise around to Virgo, the last sign before the autumn equinox, at the lower right. Thus, below Mithras at the bottom of the circle and at the beginning and end of the sequence are the points of the spring and autumn equinoxes;[83] above him at the summit (and emphasized by his right hand which here reaches up to touch the circle) is the point of the summer solstice where Gemini ends and Cancer starts.

The primary division of the Trier rock-birth is thus quite different from that of the Housesteads rock-birth. But the Trier rock-birth is a more complex composition that the Housesteads.[84] In the latter it was the central upright of Mithras' body that called attention to the balanced semicircles of solar and lunar houses to right and left. In the Trier relief, however, Mithras' body is tilted to one side, as he leans back and gazes upwards. The line of his body is thus on a diagonal, *and the point to which it leads is the boundary between Cancer and Leo* (see diagram, fig. 3). Thus, in both monuments — and they are the only two of their kind to have the zodiac — the Cancer-Leo boundary is directly over Mithras' head. This is surely more than coincidence. For this scene, and for whatever it means, that boundary point is somehow privileged and significant.

What might that significance be? One must bear in mind that it is *not* the point of the summer solstice, which would seem the obvious point to place over Mithras' head. The solstice, depending on the astrological or astronomical system used,[85] lies either at the *start* of Cancer (i.e. the Gemini-

---

[83] There could be no neater way, incidentally, of rendering iconographically the difficult doctrine, recorded by Porphyry (*De antro* 24) that Mithras has his "proper seat" (οἰκείαν καθέδραν) assigned at the equinox*es* (κατὰ τὰς ἰσημερίας): one setting but two points in space — and those diametrically opposite each other. By halving his zodiac but retaining the form of a complete ring, the designer of the Trier relief conflates the two equinoxes in a single place, which he makes coincide with the rock base from which Mithras is born.

[84] In addition to the figure of Mithras and the zodiac, the Trier monument has elements which the Housesteads monument does not have. Outside the zodiac, at four corners, are wind gods; below, set against the rocky base, are the attendant animals of the bull-killing: (r. to l.) dog, snake, raven. One is reminded that in their celestial form these are the paranatellonta of the summer signs privileged for representation in the partial zodiac (see above, p. 20 with n. 46 *ad fin.*). Conspicuously absent is the scorpion — but then Scorpius is one of the signs *not* included in the partial zodiac. The whole scene of wind gods, zodiac, rock-birth and animals is framed in an *aediculum*, on the tympanum of which are represented (l. to r.) a lion and a snake-encircled crater (further relevant constellation symbols!), a thunderbolt, a globe with crossed zones, and a mass of rock (the last two misdescribed in *CIMRM*). The ensemble in the tympanum might also be seen as symbols of the four elements. Above, to left and right in their usual Mithraic locations are busts of Sol and Luna. Finally, Mithras carries in his left hand a globe, no doubt symbolic of his world rule (his right hand, as we have seen, touches and [?] supports the zodiac at its summit). Notable is the absence of the usual implements of the rock-birth, i.e. the sword and the torch.

[85] The alternatives are discussed by Neugebauer (above, n. 7), 2.593-600.

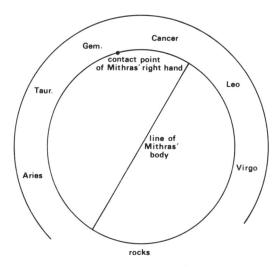

Fig. 3. *Composition of the zodiac of the Trier rock-birth (CIMRM 985)*

Cancer boundary) or at some degree *within* Cancer, but never at the end. The significance of the Cancer-Leo boundary rests therefore on something more recherché. I offer two suggestions. The first is the more relevant to the present study, for it once again involves the planets. There was an astrological theory that the great "return" (ἀποκατάστασις) of the planets to a single point of longitude would take place in Cancer. It would be accompanied by universal conflagration or deluge or both.[86] A version of this theory, attributed to Antiochus,[87] an astrologer probably of the first century B.C.,[88] is specific on the precise location: "The cosmic recurrence takes place in 1,753,005 years; then all the stars come together in the 30th [i.e. the last] degree of Cancer or the first of Leo, and a complete fulfilment[89] occurs." The Cancer-Leo boundary, in other words, is the point reached by all the planets at the end of the world. By placing that point at the apex of the composition, the Housesteads designer, I suggest, makes allusion to the end of things in a monument which depicts, in the birth of Mithras, their beginning.

My second suggestion has to do with the entry and exit of souls to and from the world. We know that the Mysteries were much interested in that question (Porphyry *De antro* 21-28, Origen *Contra Celsum* 6.22).[90] In astrological

---

[86] Seneca *Nat. Quaest.* 3.29.1 (citing Berossus) assigns the deluge to a grand conjunction in Capricorn, the conflagration to the conjunction in Cancer.

[87] *Cat. Cod. Astr. Gr.* 1.163 (Rhetorius).

[88] W. and H. G. Gundel, *Astrologumena* (Wiesbaden 1966), 115.

[89] Or, reading ἐκπύρωσις for ἐκπλήρωσις, "conflagration."

[90] Note esp. *De antro* 6: "It is by leading the *mystes* [μυσταγωγοῦντες: the very literal translation is intentional] through the descent and return of souls that the Persians initiate him."

lore the usual place of entry is Cancer or the summer solstice and of exit
Capricorn or the winter solstice.[91] But there is a variant reported by Varro (*ap.*
Servius *ad. Georg.* 1.34) who attributes it to one Empedotimus:[92] "Varro says
that he had read that for a certain Empedotimus of Syracuse the limitations of
mortal vision had been cleared away and that he had seen, among other
things, three gates and three routes: one in the sign of Scorpius, where Her-
cules was said to have passed to the gods, *another at the boundary (limitem)
between Leo and Cancer*, and a third between Aquarius and Pisces." I suggest
that for the Mysteries too the Cancer-Leo boundary served as an access point
to and from the heavens, and that is why it is privileged in its setting in our
two rock-births. It is the esoteric access point, and it did not exclude the more
publicly known point in Cancer or at the solstice; for the Mysteries also incorporated the latter into their doctrine (*De antro* 24),[93] and indeed the Trier
monument seems to allude to both: the Cancer-Leo gate above Mithras' head
(as also in the Housesteads scene), the Gemini-Cancer gate at the apex of the
composition and marked by Mithras' hand.

VII

The preceding section was in the nature of an excursus, intended to
demonstrate further the incorporation of learned astrology into the monument of the Mysteries, and in particular the exploitation of the system of
"houses" as a mode of relating the signs of the zodiac to the planets and thus
alluding to both simultaneously. We now return to the main line of our discussion and to the last major monument to be introduced, the upper register of
the Ottaviano Zeno monument. Like certain other reliefs, it carries a row of
altars. But it has, in addition, two strategically placed figures, and these open

---

[91] Porph. *De antro* 21 ff., Macrobius *In somn.* 1.12.1-2, Proclus *In remp.* 2.128 f. (Kroll). The
proximate source is Numenius, but others may lie behind him — including at least the Mithraists
(*De antro* 24; and see below). On Porphyry, Macrobius and Proclus, and on their relationship to
each other and to Numenius, see (*inter alios*) H. De Ley, *Macrobius and Numenius: A Study of
Macrobius in Somn.*, I, *c.* 12 (Coll. Latomus, Brussels 1972). The scholarship on that topic is considerable, but since its problems are not at issue here I omit further references.

[92] Empedotimus seems to be a fictitious character, like Plato's Er, a visionary invented as a
vehicle for other-worldly truths; his inventor, Heraclides of Pontus: E. Rohde, *Psyche*, 7-8 ed.
(Tübingen 1921) 2.94 f., n. 1; also I. Culianu (above, n. 12), 40 f.; H. B. Gottschalk, *Heraclides
of Pontus* (Oxford 1980), 98 ff.

[93] Disputed by R. Turcan in *Mithras Platonicus* (above, n. 74), 88 f. The question is a complex
one which I shall address elsewhere, since it is marginal to the present study of the planets in
Mithraism. Confirmation that the theory of gates of descent and ascent in the solstitial signs is
Mithraic will depend on demonstrating (i) that the theory is an integral part of the indisputably
Mithraic doctrine of the seat of Mithras at the equinoxes, and not incompatible with it, as claimed
by Turcan; (ii) that it is in fact exemplified in the monuments, both in the icons and in the
mithraea. We shall see (below, pp. 92 ff.) an example of the latter in the Barberini fresco. Mean-
while, let the question remain open.

up the possibility of deciphering for the altars a planetary order — or orders. The work, however, is lost, and reconstructing as nearly as possible its exact appearance must be our first task — by no means a straightforward one.

As mentioned already (n. 49; see also n. 50), the Ottaviano Zeno monument was for long known only from drawings which reproduced its design. Recently, the main part, the immediate bull-killing scene, was located in São Paulo, Brasil) and correctly identified by M. J. Vermaseren, who published it as his *Mithriaca IV* (see above, n. 49). The general accuracy of the copies with respect to this recovered part confirms the genuineness of the still missing upper register. This is as well, for the register is quite unique and one might otherwise have suspected that at least some of its details were artists' fantasies. The drawings are amply reproduced and their lineage traced in Vermaseren's monograph, and the upper register is discussed in full together with the recovered main scene.

The upper register, it seems, was a separate block of stone. It will have been mounted on the wall above the main relief.[94] That it is part of what is essentially a single composition is suggested by the presence of Sol and Luna in the upper register and their absence from the main stone. Since the main scene contains all the other elements of a full tauroctony (together with one or two unusual ones — see below) it is most improbable that the luminaries were omitted: the upper register may therefore be supposed to have supplied the deficiency.[95]

While the general appearance of the upper register can be accepted as known, its dimensions and even its precise shape and full contents remain problematic. All but one of the drawings show an elongated rectangle directly above the main scene but extending slightly beyond the latter's left border. Also, the left end of the register appears damaged, broken off with a jagged diagonal. Here it is important to note that all these drawings (with the one ex-

---

[94] There are no traces of sockets, etc., for attachment on the upper surface of the main stone (Vermaseren [above, n. 49], 23). If the upper register rested directly on the main stone it will have fitted behind Mithras' cap which obtrudes above the upper margin of the main relief. It cannot be assumed that the two reliefs necessarily graced the end wall of the cult niche. The main stone, despite its detail, is quite small (only a quarter of a meter in height and width). Conceivably, then, the pair may not have been the principal icon of their mithraeum.

[95] Though slight, in my opinion, the possibility nevertheless remains that this "upper register" may have been a separate composition from somewhere else in the mithraeum or even from another site. That it is not Mithraic at all is improbable in the extreme: though unique in form and combination, its elements are all Mithraic — Sol, Luna, altars and, especially, the two snake-encircled figures. See Vermaseren (above, n. 49), Ch. 1 on the probable provenance and history of these and related monuments. Nothing in that history makes it in any way likely that the upper register was not from the same mithraeum as the main scene of the Ottaviano Zeno monument. In the arguments which follow, little actually depends on the relationship of main scene and upper register (although of course much — indeed everything — depends on the Mithraic nature of the latter); that little may be discounted by readers who are not convinced that the two parts belong together.

ception, to which we shall return below) are but a single witness, deriving ultimately from the original of A. Lefréry's print of 1564.[96] Now this archetypal drawing was demonstrably out of scale. We know this because the stone of the main scene is not the only part to have been recovered. The pair of independent reliefs of the torchbearers have also been found — on an earlier occasion, in Paris, and also by M. J. Vermaseren (see above, no. 50 *ad fin.*). These are shown in the drawings one above the other on the left, which was perhaps how they were positioned in the Zeno collection when the original drawing was made. In the drawings their combined height is equal to that of the main scene; and yet we now know that each relief of a torchbearer was individually taller than the relief of the main scene: 0.33 m compared to 0.27 m. The relationship of the different reliefs on the drawings is thus found to be a matter of the composition of the archetypal drawing itself rather than of the actual monuments. We cannot know, then, whether the upper register was in fact somewhat longer than the width of the main stone or whether the artist merely extended it to fill some of the vacant space above his rendering of the two torchbearers. Likewise, we cannot know exactly what elements in the upper register were aligned above what in the main scene. Was the winged figure in the former directly above the tauroctonous Mithras in the latter, as the drawings — again with the same single exception — show them? One cannot say with certainty. Lastly, was the ratio of sizes approximately as in the drawings? It is most unlikely that there was the same magnitude of discrepancy as we find with the torchbearers, since it is fairly certain that the upper register belongs with the main scene as part of a single composition, while the torchbearers were probably from elsewhere in the mithraeum (see above, n. 50). Nevertheless, the possibility of some degree of difference must be allowed.

There are doubts, too, about the upper register's rectangular shape. One of the drawings, the exception alluded to above, shows its contents arranged in a semicircular arc. This work, which there is reason to suppose is independent of all the other drawings and derives from a different and earlier autopsy (see

---

[96] See Vermaseren (above, n. 49), 7 ff. with Plates 11-17. Lafréry's print (Vermaseren, Pl. 12) is from his *Speculum Romanae Magnificentiae* (Rome), an album of prints of various dates issued in many editions with different contents: see Chr. Huelsen, "Das *Speculum Romanae Magnificentiae* des Antonio Lafreri," in *Collectanea Variae Doctrinae* (Festschrift Leo S. Olschki, Munich 1921), 121-170, no. 66, p. 156. Vermaseren (pp. 7 f. with Pl. 11) attaches equal weight to the drawing — it is actually the only one not in printed form — in the collection of the sixteenth-century Dutch humanist Pighius. But that drawing has at the end of the accompanying allegorical explication and key — the explication is virtually identical with Lafréry's — a sentence to the effect that Joachim Camerarius [the Younger] "adduces" (*adducit*) this illustration in his *De re rustica* of 1577. As far as I can tell, there is no reason to suppose that the explication with its final sentence does not belong to the original execution of the drawing. The Pighius drawing thus appears to be copied from Camerarius who in turn borrowed it from Lafréry. Although important for the history of the monuments, the 1562 and thus pre-Lafréry description of Aldroandi (see Vermaseren, pp. 1 ff.) contributes nothing to the elucidation of the upper register.

below), reproduces the design of a lost intaglio which was in turn modelled on the Ottaviano Zeno monument.[97] Now the oval shape of the gem stone would surely be sufficient in itself to account for the semicircular form of the upper register as it appears around the top of the intaglio. However, the shape of the recovered stone of the main relief does admit a possibility — though, in my view, only a slight one — that the upper register was not in fact a straight bar in form as the other drawings represent it. The top of the recovered stone does not follow a single straight horizontal line; it lacks a triangular section from its upper right corner. The cut is regular, and although it might have been made at a later date it could equally well have been part of the original shaping of the stone in the cutting of the relief. Vermaseren combines this datum with the semicircular arrangement of the elements of the upper register on the intaglio to suggest that the upper register itself was perhaps curved and that its ends lapped round into the vacant upper corners of the main stone.[98] In the first place, however, as I have suggested, the oval form of the intaglio is alone enough to account for the composition of the upper register upon it: the register has been distorted merely in order to occupy the given rim of the gem stone. In the second place, it is most unlikely that a similar triangular corner was lacking from the upper left of the original main stone. The left side of the main scene is of course still lost, but *both* the surviving part *and* the drawings suggest that the composition required the full space of the upper left corner for Mithras' billowing mantle (together with the raven) if the garment was not to be absurdly and untypically truncated — as it is on the intaglio. The main stone was thus probably irregular even in its original form:

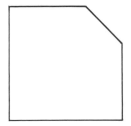

This is reflected in the rectangular drawings by the corresponding white space and notable absence of content in the upper right.[99] It is accordingly most

---

[97] See Vermaseren (above, n. 49), 21-24 with Pl. 25.

[98] *Id.* 23.

[99] But it is peculiar that the rectangular drawings should show the missing and broken left edge of the upper register while ignoring the triangular spandrel left out of the upper right corner of the main stone. I can only suggest that while the artist of the archetype had no interest in the *regular* framework of the reliefs — the drawings suppress it almost completely — he wished nevertheless to indicate where there was some damage and loss from the margins.

unlikely that the upper register would have lapped down into one corner, the right, while continuing level over the other, the left.

Finally, we come to the contents of the upper register. All the drawings show, in standard Mithraic fashion, Sol with his quadriga on the left, Luna with her biga on the right. Between them extend a row of seven burning altars interspersed with swords. The intaglio simplified the altars to mere flames and suppressed the swords.[100] The row of altars above the main scene is likewise Mithraic, being particularly a feature of Danubian reliefs. Immediately to the left of the row of altars is a human figure encircled by a snake. Another snake-entwined figure, winged and holding a long sceptre, stands between the third and fourth altars from the left. All these elements are shown diagrammatically in fig. 4.

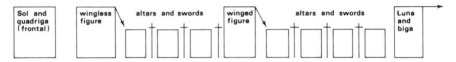

Fig. 4. *Upper register of the Ottaviano Zeno monument* (*CIMRM* 335: excluding possible elements of the "water miracle" on the left)

So far unanimity between the drawings prevails. But the drawing of the intaglio now introduces an extra element. Between Sol and the wingless figure it places a naked person, kneeling on one knee and with his arms raised before him, in front of a vertical mass of rock or flame and surrounded by nine stars.[101] The other drawings show nothing there and no room for anything; and their archetype is in general demonstrably more reliable than the intaglio. Is this extra element then a fantasy, invented and added by the artist of the intaglio for balance? Two factors sugges that it is not. First, there is the broken left end of the upper register shown in the rectangular drawings. A plausible scenario might be that the artist of the intaglio (or his source) saw the monument *before* the break was made in the upper register, recorded an element that was genuinely present, but transposed it with Sol for the very good reason of effecting a balance between the two luminaries at either end.[102] The second

---

[100] It is agreed that the intaglio is certainly in error here: see Vermaseren (above, n. 49), 22. Daggers alternate with altars (and other symbols) on *CIMRM* 1973: see above, n. 27. See also Vermaseren, p. 50.

[101] Vermaseren ([above, n. 49], 23) gives eight, Cumont (*TMMM* 2.451 f., "Pierres gravées et amulettes" no. 11) seven, but the reproduction (Vermaseren, Pl. 25) clearly shows nine, including one just above the person's left knee.

[102] The designer of the intaglio is demonstrably concerned with balance. Note what appears to be his taking of the torches of the torchbearers from the separate panels and his placement of them to right and left below Sol and Luna. They there echo, though with a clever inversion, the torches leaning against the trees in the main scene. A further argument from balance likewise suggests that the kneeling figure was no invention. The designer places at the summit of the oval the

factor makes this plausible scenario quite likely. As Cumont notes (see above, n. 101), the kneeling figure and the mass in front of him bear a striking resemblance to a part of the Mithraic scene of the "water miracle": Mithras shoots an arrow at a rock before which kneels a person with outstretched hands. It is hard to imagine that, had the kneeling figure and the rock not been present, a seventeenth-century or earlier designer would by happy coincidence have imported something so appropriately Mithraic, especially considering that that particular scene was just not accessible on the monuments then known in western Europe.[103] One concludes, then, that the intaglio probably does derive from a separate and earlier autopsy of the monument than Lafréry's print, and that the element of the kneeling figure is genuine though misplaced. If that is so, then there is a further implication which has not yet received comment. The scene as represented on the gem stone is deficient: there is no equivalent of the shooting Mithras. But surely the artist behind the intaglio would not have taken one figure without the other. One must conclude, then, that the upper register was *already* damaged when this artist saw it: Mithras to the left of the kneeling figure was no longer there.

The presence of the water miracle, if we may tentatively accept it, suggests Danubian influence — I would not go so far as to say provenance — on the composition of the upper register; for it is in that location in the upper left that we find the water miracle typically on Danubian monuments. Moreover, the arrangement implied by the intaglio is the same: left to right — Mithras shooting, then the figure kneeling towards the right with outstretched hands, then the rock.[104] Danubian too, as we have noted, is the row of seven altars on the upper register, as indeed is the very concept of an upper register as a distinct unit of composition. Finally, a curious detail in the composition of Sol and Luna has its only certain parallel in a Danubian relief. There is an imbalance between the two luminaries; for while Luna in regular fashion drives her biga off to the right, Sol and his team are shown frontally, driving as it were directly at the viewer. The only Mithraic monument which is definitely the same in this respect is the recently discovered relief from Intercisa (Dunaújváros) in Pannonia.[105] These Danubian links would not be of much

---

three flames (his substitute for the altars) between the snake-encircled figures. To the right are the remaining four flames, and then Luna. Had the designer needed to invent a corresponding filler on the left, he would probably have blocked in four more flames before Sol. The kneeling figure is distinctly asymmetric, and for that reason as well likely to be genuine.

[103] See Vermaseren (above, n. 49), 22-24.

[104] See, e.g., *CIMRM* 1740, 1815, 1920, 1935, 1958, 1972, 2018, 2023, 2051, 2214, 2338. Frequently there is a second (standing) person behind Mithras, i.e. on the far left of the scene.

[105] Illustrated in *JMS* 1.2 (1976), Pl. 6. Interestingly, as on the Ottaviano Zeno monument, horses have been substituted for the usual oxen on Luna's biga. The teams of Sol and Luna may have been shown in similar poses on the fragmentary Königshoffen relief (*CIMRM* 1359). For other details of the iconography of Sol and Luna see Vermaseren (above, n. 49), 51.

significance were it not for the fact that, of the two monuments with the busts of the planetary gods, one, the Brigetio plate (*CIMRM* 1727: above, pp. 17 f.) is definitely Danubian, and the other, the Bologna relief (693: above, p. 19 with n. 40) shows at least strong Danubian influence. The seven altars on the Ottaviano Zeno monument are clearly planetary and the two snake-encircled figures that accompany them suggest that something more precise and complex is intended than a simple allusion to the assemblage of the seven. It is thus of some interest that the same regional affiliations with the Danube area can be demonstrated for the Ottaviano Zeno monument as for the two monuments of the tauroctony that carry symbols of the planets in explicitly identifiable forms and orders.[106]

It is of course the presence of the two snake-encircled figures that allows the possibility of deciphering a planetary order (or orders) and a particular meaning (or meanings) for the row of altars on the Ottaviano Zeno monument. The placement of the figures is clearly significant, for it throws out of balance the otherwise symmetrical sequence of the seven altars alternating with the six swords and flanked by Sol and Luna. The two figures seem to be related to particular altars, since they are both angled slightly to the (viewer's) right and appear to be looking inwards and downwards, the wingless figure to the first altar on the left, the winged figure to the fourth and central altar. The figures thus preside over, or are in some way to be identified with, the beginning or end and the mid point of whatever sequence or sequences the altars symbolize.

It would seem logical, then, to try to identify the two figures in order to decipher the order of the planets intimated on the monument. Nevertheless, that approach would, I believe, be quite mistaken. Too often in the scholarship on the Mysteries we have rushed to establish facile identities: this figure or this symbol is this deity — with the fatal correlative that it therefore cannot be another.[107] But the enigma of the person of Mithras at the core of the

---

[106] It is significant too that the Ottaviano Zeno monument, on its main scene, shows the secondary attributes of the torchbearers, the bull's head and scorpion, as does the Bologna tauroctony: above, pp. 25 f. with n. 50. This detail, indeed, appears from its other occurrences to be mainly Danubian: above, pp. 26 f. I have played with the idea that fitted into the area of the deficient upper right corner of the main relief, and to balance the water miracle on the left, there might have been a representation of the birth of Mithras from the rock, either as part of the original main stone which was then broken off and the edge subsequently straightened and smoothed, or as a small separate stone (or even as a pendant on the right of the upper register). This is certainly the place for the rockbirth in Danubian compositions and it occurs there in another Roman relief of demonstrably Danubian affinities, *CIMRM* 556 (see H. Lavagne, "Les reliefs mithriaques à scènes multiples en Italie," in *Mélanges de philosophie, de littérature et d'histoire offerts à Pierre Boyancé* [Coll. de l'Ec. franç. de Rome 22, Paris 1974], 481-504, at 487 f.). The supposition would also solve the puzzle of a seemingly vacant area in an otherwise full, indeed cluttered, composition. But it is, of course, entirely speculative.

[107] I hazard the opinion that the principal victim of the will-o'-the-wisp of aiming to pin down the Mysteries' theology, god by god, was Cumont himself: see esp. sect. ix of Ch. 5 of *TMMM* 1. What misled Cumont, I believe, was in general his overly sanguine assumption that the analysis of

Mysteries should have warned us that this is wrong. Mithras both is and is not the Sun: is, because scores of inscriptions call him such: is not, because in the iconography Sol is a separate person with a separate story. Similarly, there are pointers on the Ottaviano Zeno monument which suggest that to ask *who* the snake-encircled figures are is to ask the wrong question. For immediately one is faced with a paradox. On the one hand, the row of altars obviously symbolizes the planets. On the other hand, and just as obviously, the two figures, related to particular altars, do not correspond to particular planetary gods in any known guise. Furthermore, it is not certain that we are in fact dealing with two figures — and thus with separate identities — at all. The basic iconography and stance of each is the same: a naked anthropomorphic being, wrapped in four serpentine coils, gazing down at an altar to his left. It is merely that one has adjuncts which the other does not, namely wings and a sceptre.[108] Possibly, then, the two are one and the same, but at different stages in a sequence or process; or perhaps even personifications of two stages within a single process, its beginning or end and its mid point. The winged and sceptred figure might thus represent the acquisition of what was not possessed at the start; alternatively, the wingless and sceptreless figure might represent the loss or renunciation of what was possessed in mid course. Finally, one must bear in mind the very real possibility, to be discussed later, that more than a

a religion would yield the sort of precise and definite results that one might expect from the subjects of scientific enquiry, and in particular the need to find equivalents for the deities of the Iranian pantheon which his premise that Mithaism was the Roman form of Mazdaism demanded. See R. L. Gordon's critique in "Franz Cumont and the Doctrines of Mithraism," *Mithraic Studies*, 215-248, esp. 221-225. Cumont's attempt at the two figures on the Ottaviano Zeno monument (*TMMM* 2, no. 70) strikes me as typical not only of his positivist approach but also of the implausibility into which that approach sometimes leads. For Cumont the central figure is necessarily Aion, for all such figures are types of the god who is the counterpart of the Iranian time god Zurvān. What then of the second figure? Since it is redundant to Cumont's theological scheme, it is dismissed as an artist's mistake. But a mistake for what? Now the second figure is next to Sol, and Sol on the monuments is occasionally accompanied by a Phosphorus. So the original figure misinterpreted by the sixteenth-century artist, Cumont suggested, was probably a Phosphorus. Yet the figure in the drawings is quite unlike a Phosphorus, and it is well-nigh impossible to see how an artist making a reasonably faithful copy could have rendered the latter as the former. Incidentally, a consequence of Cumont's hypothesis here would necessarily be that the intaglio has no independent value as a witness to the original monument; for it is inconceivable that two artists, i.e. Lafréry's and the designer of the intaglio, independently derived the same figure from autopsy of a Phosphorus. Hence the intaglio would have to have been derived from Lafréry's design (or from one of the drawings within the same tradition of rectangular composition). Consequently, the kneeling figure on the intaglio would reflect not a part of a genuine water miracle on the original relief but a fantasy of the intaglio's designer. Since, for reasons argued above, that final implication is unlikely, one should rather suppose that the intaglio is indeed based on independent autopsy and therefore that the wingless figure on the original relief was essentially as we see it in the drawings. Finally, it is surely methodologically sounder to accept the modified repetition of the snake-encircled figure as a reality and to try to explain it than to dismiss it *a priori*.

[108] Vermaseren, in a sensible and restrained discussion ([above, n. 49], 52 f.), rightly introduces this possibility: "... deux figures différentes du même dieu ..."

single planetary order is intimated in the row of altars. If that is so, then the two figures will likely shift their meanings as the orders shift, and to posit a single pair of identities would hopelessly obscure the dynamics of the monument.

A safer approach is therefore simply to relate the figures to whatever we find in the Mysteries that is iconographically similar and especially to whatever we find in analogous locations on the monuments — to proceed, in effect, from context, structure and associations.[109] This will not answer the question of who these persons are. It is, however, a necessary concomitant of our principal task, which is to explore the planetary sequence or sequences implicit in the row of altars to which the figures are related.

The two figures are clearly types of that strange being whose statue has been recovered from a number of mithraea, and whose most persistent iconographic trait is the snake spiralling round and up the body. I propose generally to speak of him, no doubt rather cumbrously, in just those terms as the "snake-encircled figure."[110] For to use any of the proposed identifications, such as Aion, Zurvān or Arimanius/Ahriman,[111] would be tendentious, and the neutral descriptive term, coined from his *second* most common feature, the "leontocephaline" or "lion-headed" god,[112] would be paradoxical in the

---

[109] A model of this sort of approach through iconography, placement and juxtaposition is Vermaseren's perceptive article "The Miraculous Birth of Mithras" (above, n. 81), esp. 292 ff. where he explores types of Saturn and Oceanus. Implicit in Vermaseren's treatment is the supposition that the identities of the gods are not fixed but flow into and out of each other.

[110] Or the "snake-encircled power" or "... god," although this of course begs an ontological question, or at least a question of status.

[111] Given my premises, it would clearly be beside the point to confront here the scholarly literature on who the god is. A useful survey is given in J. R. Hinnells, "Reflections on the Lion-Headed Figure in Mithraism," *Monumentum H. S. Nyberg* I = *Acta Iranica*, Ser. 2, 1 (Leiden 1975), 333-369, an article which has the further merit of presenting, with statistical diagrams, all the nuances of the figure's iconography. For a brief account of the issues and controversies see also my "Mithraism since Franz Cumont" (above, n. 4), 2086-89. Vermaseren, in his treatment of the god in the context of the Ottaviano Zeno monument (see above, n. 108), is wisely catholic in admitting all manner of possibilities: "La personnalité de cette divinité est ... très complexe. Elle doit être mise en rapport ... avec Saturne, Sérapis, Phanès, Pluton et Kronos, Caelus et Océanus." Likewise in his "A Magical Time God" (*Mithraic Studies* 446-456), where the god's temporal aspects are stressed (as also by R. Melkelbach, *Mithras* [above, n. 4], 224-226). Similarly broad in interpretation is J. Duchesne-Guillemin: these figures, whether lion- or human-headed, "ne sont donc que deux variations sur le thème de l'identité Aiōn-Sarapis-Zeus-Hélios-Mithra-Hadès-Ahriman etc." ("Aiōn et le léontocéphale, Mithra et Ahriman," *La Nouvelle Clio* 10-12 [1958-62], 91-98, at 97). A realization of the figure's complexity is the first step. What will need exploration in future scholarship is the *function* of the figure in each of its roles, the significance of the various equations, and why, finally, Mithraism needed that degree of complexity.

For a catalogue of the monuments with full illustrations (but little discussion), see now M. Le Glay, "Aion," *Lexicon Iconographicum Mythologiae Classicae* 1.1 (Zürich and Munich 1981), 399-411.

[112] Hinnells (above, n. 111) gives 33 instances of the snake as attribute and 26 of the lion's head (Diagram A, p. 368; Diagram B, p. 369, which represents, in Hinnells's opinion, "only those monuments on which ... any interpretation of the figure can be based," gives 21 instances of each feature).

present context of the Ottaviano Zeno figures and, furthermore, inappropriate as excluding some rather important exemplars.[113] Again, I caution that we are not necessarily dealing with a single being or person — still less with something as definite as an individual god — though the constraints of discourse force one to speak in those terms. Rather, we have to do with a complex of shifting but linked ideas expressed in a set of iconographically related images.

Although the snake-encircled figure most often appears in the form of a free-standing statue or self-contained relief (the former sometimes of considerable size), it is occasionally found on the cult icon. In *CIMRM* 2320 (a fragment from Serdica) it appears in the bottom left corner, to the left of the usual trio of scenes that occupy the lower register.[114] However, in the fresco of the Barberini Mithraeum (*CIMRM* 390),[115] and perhaps also in one of the lost fragments of *CIMRM* 1510 (the major relief from Mithraeum II at Poetovio: see above, n. 68), its position is analogous to that of the winged figure in the Ottaviano Zeno monument, for it occupies the centre of the upper part of the icon. The Barberini figure we have met already (above, pp. 32 ff.; diagram, fig. 5, p. 91). It too is found within a set of altars; there are three on either side, and, as we observed, the figure's head either obscures a central seventh or itself *is* that central seventh. We inferred that the Barberini figure and its altar are thus equivalent to the bust in the centre of the planetary sequence at the top of the Bologna relief (*CIMRM* 693), which is that of Jupiter-Serapis.[116] Thence it may be related to the solar Serapis in an analogous location on the larger Dura tauroctony (*CIMRM* 40: above, p. 33);[117] also, by position and the fact that the figure's head is probably leonine here in the Barberini Mithraeum (see above, n. 65) and certainly so in numerous other instances, to the lion's mask in the upper centre of the Danubian relief *CIMRM* 2198 (above, p. 32). To the complex so formed we may now add the winged snake-encircled figure linked to the central altar of the upper register of the Ottaviano Zeno monument. In the accompanying table three other possible

---

[113] E.g. the figure from Mérida, *CIMRM* 777. See also above, n. 64, on the Barberini figure.

[114] Also to be mentioned is the figure found in the lower right corner of several Danubian reliefs (e.g. *CIMRM* 1935, 1958, 1972, 2291) hailing (?) the ascending chariot of Sol and Mithras. Its pose is quite different, for it is reclining rather than standing; but it does carry our figure's principal iconographic trait, the snake encircling the body. Significantly, its pose and location link it both with the reclining Saturn and with Oceanus. See esp. G. Sfameni Gasparro, "Il mitraismo nell'ambito della fenomenologia misterica," *Mysteria Mithrae*, 299-348, at 318 f.

[115] On this monument, see now the new description, analyses and colour plates in M. J. Vermaseren, *Mithriaca* III (above, n. 64), esp. pp. 84-87 on the snake-encircled figure and its surroundings.

[116] See, however, n. 64 (above) and Appendix on the question of the authenticity of the Jupiter-Serapis bust.

[117] See above, n. 67, on the possibility that the London and Sa. Prisca Serapis heads were similarly positioned.

members have also been added, but in parentheses. For the certain members the significant iconographic and contextual details are given in the column on the right. One should note that the Ottaviano Zeno monument breaks the pattern in one very important respect. In all the other instances there is a triadic structure (see above, p. 34 with diagram) in which Sol and Luna balance each other on the flanks (with or without intervening elements separating them from the main figure). On the Ottaviano Zeno monument, however, the inclusion of the wingless snake-encircled figure to the right of Sol in association with the first (or last) altar obliterates both triad and balance and creates, if anything, an asymmetric quartet.[118]

The snake-encircled figure and related elements at the top centre of the tauroctony

Monument	Element	Iconography and context
Barberini	snake-encircled figure	lion-headed (probably — see n. 65) stands on globe in centre of set of planetary altars, at ends of which Luna (r.) and Sol (l.) in centre of zodiac
Ottaviano Zeno	snake-encircled figure	human headed winged and carries sceptre in centre of set of planetary altars, at ends of which are Luna (r.) and Sol (l.) wingless snake-encircled figure between Sol and far left altar
Bologna	Jupiter-Serapis	iconography of Serapis (but see Appendix) in centre of sequence of busts of planetary gods in week-day order from Moon (r.) to Sun (l.) hence, by position, Jupiter
Dura	Serapis	*kalathos* solar rays in centre of zodiac originally formed triad with Sol (r.) and Luna (l.)
CIMRM 2198	lion's head	Luna (r.), Sol (l.)
(? Poetovio II	snake-encircled figure	see n. 68)
(? Sa. Prisca	Serapis	see n. 67)
(? London	Jupiter-Serapis	see n. 67)

---

[118] The water miracle on the extreme left throws the composition still further out of balance.

Let us turn now to the iconography of the snake-encircled figure[119] and the various meanings to which it gives expression, especially as we find it in the context of the Barberini and Ottaviano Zeno monuments. In some measure its significance will remain conjectural, but that should be no real impediment. What we seek is a coherent pattern of ideas rather than a precise set of equations.

On the Barberini fresco, as in several other works,[120] the snake-encircled figure stands on a globe, which clearly symbolizes the cosmos — and power over the cosmos. The globe on the Barberini fresco still bears traces of the oblique zone of the zodiac, which is echoed — significantly, I believe — in the slanting bands of the snake's coils.[121] This astronomical motif is more emphatically expressed on the Roman relief *CIMRM* 543. Here the globe carries, in ample proportions, the zones of both equator and zodiac, intersecting in the form of the chi cross on the model of Plato's *Timaeus*, where they denote the two world motions, that of the stars and of the universe in its entirety (the Same) and that of the Sun, Moon and other planets (the Different).[122]

Control of the great astronomical constituents and processes of the cosmos seems to be intimated both by the iconography of the snake-encircled figure and by its contexts. We have seen that it is set in the middle of the row of planetary altars on the Barberini fresco and that in its two manifestations on the Ottaviano Zeno monument it is related to the central altar and to what is either the first or the last (or both?). But the planets are not the only order of celestial beings to which the snake-encircled figure is related. It is also linked — more intimately, indeed — to the zodiac. We may see this most clearly on the Barberini fresco. For the god whose head masks or is the central planet divides with the globe on which his feet rest the span of the zodiac: six signs fall away in the arc to his left, and six in the arc to his right.[123] The god thus rules both orders, that of the planets and that of the signs. Or, less concretely, he is the symbol of control over both.

The zodiac is found with other examples of the snake-encircled figure. On the Arles torso (*CIMRM* 879) the sequence of the twelve signs winds around

---

[119] For the statistical data see Hinnells (above, n. 111). There is of course a wealth of apposite material on the iconography and its interpretation in Cumont, *TMMM* 1.74 ff. Though Cumont arrives at a single identification for the god, the persona and pedigree which he traces are by no means simple.

[120] *CIMRM* 382, 543, 545, 551, 1705, 2320.

[121] Cf. the writhing snake on the globe on the apotheosis relief of the column of Antoninus Pius (D. Levi, "Aion," *Hesperia* 13 [1944], 269-314, fig. 22); also below, on the snake as a symbol of the zodiac, or, more precisely, of the movement of the time-defining bodies, Sun and Moon, along the zodiac. See also R. Merkelbach's succinct analysis of the astronomical and temporal symbolism of the snake-encircled figure's iconography: "Die Kosmogonie der Mithrasmysterien," *Eranos Jahrbuch* 34 (1965), 219-257, at 242.

[122] See above, pp. 29 f. with n. 58.

[123] The figure's exact position, at the autumn equinox, between Virgo and Libra, will be discussed later. See diagram, fig. 5.

the body in tandem with the snake. On the Villa Albani statue (545) we find the four signs that mark the seasons, the equinoctial signs of spring and autumn (Aries and Libra) on the figure's chest and the tropical signs of summer and winter (Cancer and Capricorn) on its thighs. The Modena figure (695) is surrounded by the complete zodiac in an oval frame. More allusively, the sceptre borne by the figure in 543 (see above) is wrapped in a twelve-fold spiral; again, as on the Barberini fresco, there are echoes of the serpent's spiral and an intimation that zodiac and serpent are equivalent symbols. Finally, on the Dura tauroctony (40), the Serapis head which we have found to be a congener of the snake-encircled figure is set at the centre and summit of an arciform zodiac precisely as is the Barberini figure — and at precisely the same point in the sequence of signs (see preceding note).

The zodiac, as we have remarked before, is not merely a symbol of celestial space. Since it is the path on which the Sun and the Moon travel, and since the Sun and the Moon define time by their travels thereon, the zodiac is also a symbol of time. Especially, it is a symbol of seasonal time and of the seasonal cycle, containing as it does the signs of the seasons (see above on 545). The snake-encircled figure, in its relations with the zodiac, is thus a symbol of time and the seasons — and of power over this second great dimension of the cosmos as well as over the first which is space.

The most common feature of the "snake-encircled figure" is the snake itself (see above, n. 111), winding upwards in coils round the figure's legs (which are usually positioned close together in a stiff hieratic pose)[124] and trunk; the head of the snake usually rests on the figure's head,[125] which in most cases is leonine. The snake is of course a vastly multivalent symbol in antiquity. I have explored at length some of its meanings, in particular the astronomical, in my study of the Ponza Mithraeum, where we find it prominent in the composition of the unique and exquisite zodiac which adorns the ceiling.[126] Here, then, I need only summarize those meanings and some of the evidence which goes to support them. The snake is a symbol of the zodiac, or, more precisely, of the path or journey of the Sun and the Moon — particular-

---

[124] Most often so in the more elaborate Roman (i.e. City) exemplars: see Hinnells (above, n. 111), 348. Rightly, Vermaseren ([above, n. 64], 85) places great emphasis on the relation of the figure to the zodiac — and of both to time.

[125] Not so with the two figures of the Ottaviano Zeno relief. Lafréry's drawing (Vermaseren [above, n. 49], Pl. 12), (a) for the figure on the left, shows the snake's head emerging vertically, but in profile, from behind the figure's right shoulder; (b) for the central figure, the snake's head appearing horizontally from behind and just below the right shoulder, and touching (licking?) the tip of the flame from the altar on that side, i.e. the third altar from the left. The intaglio (Vermaseren, Pl. 25) shows more or less the same arrangement, except that the snake of the central figure does not touch the flame-tip. Other drawings show other poses, but since they were all copied from the Lafréry original (see above, n. 96), their variant details are without value.

[126] "Interpreting the Ponza Zodiac," *JMS* 1 (1976), 1-19, 2 (1978), 87-147, esp. 2.107-111. See also M. J. Vermaseren, *Mithriaca II: The Mithraeum at Ponza* (*EPRO* 16.2, Leiden 1974).

ly the former — around the zodiac; hence, of the Sun itself; hence, too, since the annual voyage of the Sun and the monthly voyage of the Moon around the zodiac define time, of time itself.[127] Macrobius, in a passage explicating the snake as a solar symbol, interprets the twin serpents of Mercury's *caduceus* as an image of the intertwined paths of Sun and Moon (*Sat.* 1.19.18): *ad huius modi argumenta draconum praecipue volumen electum est propter iter utriusque sideris flexuosum.*[128] Much earlier, Euripides had used the image of the solar dragon as the leader and orchestrator of the seasons (Fr. 937 Nauck): πυριγενὴς δὲ δράκων/ὁδὸν ἡγεῖται ταῖς τετραμόρφοις/ὥραισι ζευγνὺς ἁρμονία/πλούτου πολύκαρπον ὄχημα. The same image occurs in the Orphic *Hymn to Heracles* where the god is described as δώδεκ' ἀπ' ἀντολιῶν ἄχρι δυσμῶν ἆθλα διέρπων (12.12): Heracles in his labours is a type of the solar dragon "gliding through" the twelve signs or months. "Unchanging Time" (Χρόνος ἀγήραος), which in some Orphic cosmogonies was the third "principle" (ἀρχή) after water and earth, took the form of a dragon and was called Heracles.[129] Thus, when we find, as on the Arles torso (*CIMRM* 879), the snake climbing the parallel spiral of the zodiac,[130] we are led to think of the Sun (and of the Moon and other planets) moving along that path and of time which that motion creates.[131]

[127] The snake of the Ponza zodiac has, I argued, a very precise meaning: it signifies that meeting of Sun and Moon on their interlocking paths which we know as an eclipse: *op. cit.* (preceding note), 1.9-13, 2.87-107, 135 f.

[128] Note the *caduceus* as an ancillary attribute, together with the (solar) cock, on the background of the snake-encircled figure from Fagan's Mithraeum at Ostia (*CIMRM* 312). On the snake as a symbol of the sinuous path of the Sun alone, see *Sat.* 1.17.58 (*iter suum velut flexum draconis involvit*) and 69 (the image of a snake on a statue group at Hierapolis *flexuosum iter sideris* [*sc.* the Sun's] *monstrat*). In actual fact, the Sun's course around the zodiac is not "sinuous" at all, since the Sun, alone of the planets, does not deviate from the ecliptic. It was, however, widely understood to do so; so the image of a serpentine course accurately reflects a contemporary *perception* of the Sun's path (see Pliny *N.H.* 2.67). (See, however, below on the spiral as a *correct* image of the Sun's *daily* path in the heavens.)

[129] See O. Kern, *Orphicorum Fragmenta* (2nd ed., Berlin 1963), frs. 54 (p. 130, Hieronymus and Hellanicus *ap.* Damascius), 57 (p. 137, "Orpheus" *ap.* Athenagoras), 58 (p. 138, unattrib. *ap.* Athenag.). A more specific image of time as that which devours itself is the *ouroboros*, the snake that forms a ring with its tail in its mouth (*id.* 108 f.). But the *ouroboros* is precisely *not* the type of spiralling serpent that we find on our Mithraic figure. An *ouroboros* is, however, found on a base with a Mithraic dedication, *CIMRM* 525. It is crested like a cock or basilisk (both solar symbols) and has on its tail a small lunar crescent: Sun and Moon on the zodiac thus seem to be intimated. It would be nice to suppose with *CIMRM* that the base "probably" supported a statue of the snake-encircled figure, but there are no positive indications that it did.

[130] There is a certain difficulty in that the snake is moving *against* the order of the signs; for while the snake (presumably) is climbing, the sequence of the signs descends (from Aries at the top). The Sun of course moves through the signs *in* the given order (Aries to Taurus, etc.). Is this a minor aberration, a trivial failure to match the signifier precisely to the signified, or is it a purposeful and enigmatic reversal such as the Mysteries seem to have delighted in? On the latter supposition, I suggest a possible interpretation below (n. 134).

[131] A clear example of the association of the spiralling snake with the zodiac in a non-Mithraic context is the great silver plate from Parabiago. It depicts the triumph of Cybele and Attis and is

Other qualities of the snake (real or imagined), besides its "serpentine" spiral, are also suggestive both of the Sun and of time. By shedding its skin, it rejuvenates itself, as do time and the Sun. Nonnus (*Dionys.* 41.180 ff.) speaks of the time god Aion "exchanging the burden of old age like a snake shaking off its coil of obsolete scales." Macrobius (*Sat.* 1.20.2) explains that this habit of the snake makes it an appropriate symbol of the Sun because the latter each year regains its lost altitude and power like a return from old age "to the strength of youth" (*propterea et ad ipsum solem species draconis refertur, quia sol semper velut a quadam imae depressionis senecta in altitudinem suam ut in robur revertitur iuventutis*). The spiral that we find on our Mithraic figure is peculiarly appropriate here; for as the Sun climbs from its winter nadir to its summer zenith it does in point of astronomical fact day after day follow an ascending spiral up the heavens. The snake's proverbial keenness of sight also links it with the "all-seeing" Sun, to which tie Macrobius joins an etymological argument (*Sat.* 1.20.3): the snake (*draco*) is one of the principal symbols of the Sun (*inter praecipua solis argumenta*) because it is named "ἀπὸ τοῦ δέρχειν, *id est videre*," and because it rivals the Sun "in its sharp and vigilant glance" (*acie acutissima et pervigili*). I wonder if the usual position of the snake's head at the summit of the composite Mithraic figure might not symbolize the Sun's watch over the world from its celestial vantage point.[132]

The Sun, the path of the Sun, and time are all public meanings. Perhaps the snake may also have a more esoteric significance: the passage of the soul and of the initiate. Necessarily, this is speculative, for there is no literary evidence as there is for the more overt symbolism discussed above. So one must argue in a somewhat *a priori* fashion from context and likelihood. The progress of the initiate through the grades of the Mysteries, we saw in the earlier sections of this study, was a special type of cosmic journey through the dimensions of space and time. The snake-encircled figure, it now emerges, in its iconography and setting represents the constituents of the cosmos, the great processes that take place within it, and control of those processes. It is plausible, then, to see the snake's upwards spiral as the essential symbol of the initiate's journey and progress through the realms which the snake-encircled figure represents, and

---

replete with the symbols of the elements of the cosmos: Sun and Moon (ascending and descending in quadriga and biga respectively, much as on a tauroctony), seasons, physical elements, etc. In a curious detail on the right (see Levi [above, n. 121], fig. 13) a young male figure with sceptre (Aion?) stands within (and turns?) the ring of a zodiac which is upheld by another more muscular male who is shown from the waist up emerging naked from a platform; beside the zodiac, and resting on the same platform, is an obelisk up which writhes a snake. This ensemble is obviously an allegory of time and of the powers which control and define time. On the Parabiago plate see now L. Musso, *Manifattura suntuaria e committenza pagana nella Roma del IV secolo: Il caso della Lanx di Parabiago* (Rome 1983).

[132] At another celestial summit is found another snake: the constellation Draco at the north pole. There is evidence that Draco too was identified with time and with a power that controls the cosmos: see Beck (above, n. 126), 2.115.

especially, as the Ottaviano Zeno and Barberini monuments intimate with their row of altars, through the seven planetary spheres.[133] It is also a journey through the zodiac, as the Barberini fresco and the Arles torso suggest,[134] and hence, at a more rarified level, through the dimension of time. This meaning of passage through the cosmos, we shall find, is not unsupported by other aspects of the figure's iconography.

Finally, the geometry of the snake's spiral is worth some attention. The spiral is a cylindrical helix. It is the combination in the three-dimensional (i.e. solid) world of the two simple linear forms of the two-dimensional (i.e. plane), namely the circle and the straight line:

Like the circle and the straight line, it too is "simple," for any section of it is congruent to the whole. In an Aristotelian sense, it contains both types of motion found in the universe, the rectilinear motion that characterizes things terrestrial and the circular that characterizes things celestial.[135] It is thus an elegant symbol of motion *tout court*; and if of motion, then of *process*, a process which is both cyclical and progressive. And this, as R. L. Gordon has demonstrated,[136] is precisely what characterizes initiation through the grades of the Mysteries: motifs are repeated, but at higher and higher levels. The snake's spiral, then, would be the perfect symbol of passage and initiation within the Mysteries.[137]

---

[133] This meaning, for both the snake and the figure as a whole, is divined by Hinnells ([above, n. 111], 345 f.). Hinnells seems to me correct in everything except his qualification "after death" of the "soul's ascent through the planetary spheres." R. L. Gordon, whom Hinnells cites (n. 84), is surely right in emphasizing that the planetary journey is undertaken while the initiate is still in this world. That, after all, was what the grade system and indeed the Mysteries themselves were all about: a plan for getting to heaven while still in the here and now. See now Gordon's "Reality, Evocation and Boundary in the Mysteries of Mithras" (above, n. 6) *passim*, but esp. 38 f.

[134] Here, perhaps, is a solution to the paradox posed above (n. 130) of the snake's progress *against* the order of sings on the Arles torso. Is it an enigma of reversal in the soul's journey such as we found in the inversion of the week-day planetary order at the head of the grade order (above, p. 10)? The soul, we know, enters the world *with* the order of signs (Macr. *In somn.* 1.12.4: progress from Cancer to Leo). Does the Arles torso tell us that it leaves against that order?

[135] On controversies concerning the cylindrical helix in this connection, see S. Sambursky, *The Physical World of Late Antiquity* (London 1962), 126 f.

[136] (above, n. 6), *passim*, but esp. p. 67.

[137] And note finally how on the Arles torso the helix's combination of line and circle sets the tropic (i.e. solstitial and equinoctial) signs directly one above the other in the ascending coils of the snake.

A group of less fundamental (though still significant) attributes are the sceptre, the thunderbolt and the keys.[138] These are expressive of the snake-encircled figure's cosmic power and control. The sceptre and the thunderbolt are reminiscent of Jupiter, as the instruments (together with the eagle) by which the supreme god of Graeco-Roman paganism traditionally exercises his world rule. The keys point to something more esoteric, the opening and closing of access in a process which we shall later see is passage through the planetary spheres.[139] Of the three symbols, only the sceptre is found with the figures of the Barberini or Ottaviano Zeno monuments, and that only with *one* of the Ottaviano Zeno figures. Later in our analysis we shall have to see why on the same monument one figure bears this sign of authority and the other does not. Given the indistinctness of the painting of the Barberini figure, it is not inconceivable that it might have held keys and/or a thunderbolt clutched to its chest in the usual positions for these items.[140]

As with the sceptre on the Ottaviano Zeno monument, so with the wings: the figure in the centre is winged, that on the left wingless; in due course this too will require an attempt at explanation. Wings are relatively common on the snake-encircled figure, occurring with roughly the same frequency as the keys.[141] The significance of the wings is not quite as easy to gauge as that of the preceding group. For Cumont (*TMMM* 1.83; cf. 75) they were primarily an indication of the figure's pedigree in the ancient Near East, but that is a matter of origins, not meaning. Otherwise, from the fact that there are often four of them, he linked the wings to the four winds and hence to the four corners of the world and to the four seasons. The figure from the Fagan Mithraeum, *CIMRM* 312, does indeed bear seasonal symbols on its wings. These correlations are certainly correct, but they are not exhaustive. Wings, it seems, are occasionally symbols of the Sun (Macr. *Sat.* 1.19.8, 10).[142] But of winged gods one thinks immediately of Eros, not of course the diminished erotic putto, but the great cosmological and generative figure of the Orphics, known also as Phanes or Protogonos,[143] who appears Mithraized in the famous figure at Modena (*CIMRM* 695). His wingedness (in contradistinction

---

[138] Of these, the keys are the commonest: statistics in Hinnells (above, n. 111).

[139] Access to and from the heavens is a meaning admitted by Cumont: specifically, access through the gates of descent and ascent in Cancer and Capricorn respectively, known also as the "gates of the Sun" (*TMMM* 1.83 f.).

[140] Vermaseren, in the analysis of the Barberini fresco ([above, n. 64], 85) speaks of a key in the figure's left hand, but he does not include it in the formal description (p. 13), and I can see no trace of it in the plate (no. 16).

[141] Statistics in Hinnells (above, n. 111). The Barberini figure is wingless.

[142] One must be somewhat cautious with Macrobius in this section of the *Saturnalia*. His thesis is that all gods are types of the Sun god. Thus, necessarily, *all* their attributes are solar symbols.

[143] The first of his attributes in Kern fr. 54 (above, n. 141), p. 131, are golden wings. On the Modena figure and its Orphic background, see now M. L. West, *The Orphic Poems* (Oxford 1983), 253-255.

to the traditional Greek gods, with the exception of the special case of Hermes) is the main point of relevance for his central role in the cosmogony of Aristophanes' *Birds* (690-703), and Plato (*Phaedrus* 252C-D) quotes lines from "one of the Homeridae" to the effect that in name and essence he is the "Winged One" (Πτέρωτα). The Orphic time god, whom we have already met as serpentine, was also winged.[144] Thus, the symbol of wings leads us again to cosmic power and to time.

The wings may also carry the esoteric significance of the celestial ascent of the soul. We are actually on firmer ground in assigning this meaning to the wings than to the snake, for the use of the symbolism of wings in this way can be documented from other contexts. Not merely was it a commonplace metaphor that souls were winged,[145] but Plato in the central myth of the *Phaedrus* (246-257) uses the "fact" in an elaborate way to explore the nature of the soul, its rise and fall, and of the role of love in the process. The soul is as a pair of winged horses and a charioteer. One horse is noble and disciplined, the other bad and intractable; so driving the team is a troublesome business, at least for men — the equipages of the gods are entirely orderly. Success in the handling of one's team is to soar with the gods to the heights of heaven and there to contemplate the great ideals of justice, temperance, knowledge and so forth. Failure is to lose control, to smash the wings of one's steeds or to lose them altogether. The unwinged soul falls to earth where it enters a mortal body which it animates for a time. We are all, then, unwinged souls, and our task is to grow wings again — here loves comes into play, whose pangs, for the noble lover at least, are the itch of newly sprouting wings — and to soar aloft.

In the myth of the *Phaedrus*, soul — Plato is here speaking generally — "when perfected and winged, travels the heavens and governs the cosmos" (246B-C τελέα μὲν οὖν οὖσα καὶ ἐπτερωμένη μετεωροπορεῖ τε καὶ πάντα τὸν κόσμον διοικεῖ). It is notable that the ascent of the winged souls is not merely a metaphor for moral or "spiritual" improvement (though it is that too), but also, at least in the context of the myth, a rather literal voyage to the upper reaches of the cosmos in company with the gods. That is what Mithraic initiation and the passage of the grades also was. I am not suggesting that the

---

[144] Kern fr. 54, p. 130.

[145] Personified as a young girl, the soul (Psyche) has butterfly wings: see C. C. Schlam, *Cupid and Psyche: Apuleius and the Monuments* (University Park, Pennsylvania, 1976). R. Merkelbach (*Mithras* [above, n. 4], 235-236) rightly draws attention to the three Mithraic monuments representing Psyche with Cupid as symbolizing the soul's ascent: the relief from the Capua Mithraeum (*CIMRM* 186), the fragment from the Sa. Prisca Mithraeum (Vermaseren and Van Essen [above, n. 2], 478, no. 275, Plate 128.1), and the reverse of the gem stone *CIMRM* 2356. A. M. Brizzolara ([below, n. 240], 99) correctly, I think, sees an allusion to the ascent of the soul in the winged putto as charioteer which in the Bologna relief replaces the usual scene of Mithras and Sol ascending in the latter's chariot (see above, n. 40).

Mithraists here drew explicitly on the *Phaedrus* (though it is not inconceivable),[146] only that wings were a recognized and appropriate symbol for celestial ascent and that the Mysteries so intended them on their snake-encircled figure.[147]

We come finally to the lion's head. The lion, like the snake, is a multivalent symbol. Its most obvious reference, in the context of a solar cult, is to the Sun itself.[148] The lion, in the lore of antiquity, was the Sun's animal, sharing his qualities and virtues, and serving as his earthly image.[149] As well as terrestrial lions, there is also a celestial Lion, the constellation and sign of Leo. Leo, as we saw in the context of the Housesteads birth scene, is the astrological "house" of the Sun. It is the place reached by the Sun in mid summer after the solstice. There, says Aratus, are its "hottest paths" (*Phaen.* 149; cf. Aelian *De nat. an.* 12.7); there it blazes most fiercely and triumphantly. As solar symbol, then, the lion represents the power of the Sun, a power which is both glorious and overwhelming. The latter quality is worth emphasizing. This mid-summer energy, this power of Sun-in-Lion, is anything but gentle or kindly. As a wealth of epithets attest (πυρώδης, φλογερός, καυματώδης καὶ πνιγώδης, *furibundus, siccus, rabidus, flammifer*, etc.),[150] the leonine Sun burns, consumes, destroys life. We find here, I suggest, an intimation that the process which the composite lion-headed figure represents is essentially *apogenetic*, a burning away of the things of mortal and material genesis.[151] It is no accident that the lion's head renders this strange figure formidable, indeed repellent. Along with its solar connotations, it carries too the idea of death, an association which the lion with its gaping maw or seized prey regularly conveys on funeral monuments.[152]

Within the Mysteries the lion's head will of course also intimate the Lion grade. The connotations, indeed, will be much the same as those of the

---

[146] Thus Merkelbach (see preceding note). I find it evocative, to say the least, that the winged figure on the Ottaviano Zeno monument is flanked by the chariots of the gods, namely those of Sol and Luna; also, that immediately prior to the description of soul quoted above Plato alludes to its multiformity: ἄλλοτ' ἐν ἄλλοις εἴδεσι γιγνομένη.

[147] It is strange that in his "A Suggested Interpretation of the Mithraic Lion-Man Figure" (*Etudes Mithriaques* [above, n. 68], 215-227), J. Hansman explains the figure as a Platonizing allegory of the human soul and yet does not discuss the wings and the *Phaedrus*.

[148] Note esp. the solar rays around the lion's head of *CIMRM* 103.

[149] See e.g. Aelian *De nat. an.* 12.7, Plutarch *Quaest. conviv.* 4.5.2 = *Mor.* 670C, Macr. *Sat.* 1.21.15-17, Horapollo 1.17; see also Gordon (above, n. 6), 32-37, 46 f.

[150] See W. Gundel, "Leo 9," *RE* 12.2.1973-92, at 1981 f.

[151] Of interest here is Julian's enigmatic account of the Attis myth, in the *Hymn to the Mother of the gods* (*Or.* 5, at 167), in which he has the Sun and the Lion (Leo) acting in concert in the heavens to check and limit genesis. The Lion is characterized as "the antecedent cause to the hot and fiery." He is thus jealous of Attis' dalliance with the nymph which represents descent into genesis and the dampness of matter. At the Sun's instigation, he informs on Attis, which leads to the latter's castration, interpreted as the limitation of genesis.

[152] See Hinnells (above, n. 111), 353 with n. 74 and the literature there cited.

leonine Sun, so each symbolic meaning will reinforce the other. The Mithraic Lions are associated with fire, and their function is to "consume" by fire, to cauterize genesis and so to purify.[153] The fire shovel is their symbol;[154] fiery honey, not water, is their liquid medium;[155] and according to the famous Sa. Prisca text they are the cult's incense-burners and the agents for their fellow initiates of that fiery metamorphosis which incense-burning represents:

Accipe thuricremos, Pater, accipe, sancte, Leones
per quos thuradamus, per quos consumimur ipsi.[156]

The Lions also constitute the central grade of the Mysteries. Consequently, when the snake-encircled figure is found in the centre of a sequence of seven, as it is on the Barberini and Ottaviano Zeno monuments, the grade is more explicitly signalled. The Barberini figure is probably lion-headed (see above, n. 65); but the Ottaviano Zeno figure is certainly not — in fact neither Ottaviano Zeno figure is. It might, then, be argued that the fact that the figure is given a human rather than a lion's head shows that the Lion grade is deliberately *not* signalled in this instance. I would suggest, however, the contrary: first, that the setting in the centre of the set of seven makes the actual lion's head in a sense redundant; secondly, that in a complex of symbols the absent symbol or symbols may be understood as *implied* by those present. I am aware, however, that this is treading on dangerous methodological ground. How is one to discriminate between the significant suppresion of a symbol and its casual omission because its meanings are covered by other elements or by the totality of the complex?

The Lion grade leads to the guardian of the lion grade, Jupiter. We have seen that Jupiter as supreme ruler in the old Graeco-Roman pantheon is alreay intimated in the snake-encircled figure's attributes of sceptre and thunderbolt. The same link is effected by the analogy of location, which we explored earlier (pp. 30 ff., 51 f.), between the Jupiter in the middle of the planetary busts of the Bologna relief and the snake-encircled figures in the middle of the planetary altars on the Barberini and Ottaviano Zeno monuments.

The lion's head leads to another god, who is also another planet, Saturn. Indeed, the one ancient text which can be said with a fair degree of probability actually to be speaking about the Mithraic figure suggests that Saturn was the name under which it was invoked in the Mysteries.[157] Arnobius, in a passage

---

[153] See esp. Gordon (above, n. 149).
[154] As on the Felicissimus pavement (above, p. 1).
[155] Porphyry *De antro* 15; see Gordon (above, n. 6), n. 37.
[156] Lines 16-17; on the significance of incense in this context, see Gordon, *id.* 36 f.
[157] It seems to me much more doubtful that the passage from the Third Vatican Mythographer mentioned below was derived from Mithraic material, unless at many removes.

(*Adv. nat.* 6.10, *TMMM* 2.58 f.) in which he ridicules the implausible images of various other deities known to have played a part in the theology of Mithraism (Sun, Moon, Winds), concludes: "among your gods we see the grim face of a lion smeared with pure minium and addressed by the name of crop-bearer (*nomine frugiferio*)." The appellation, Cumont argued (*TMMM* 1.77 f.), is Saturn's, and it alludes to Saturn not merely as an agricultural god, but as a god of time, equated with the N. African *Saeculum Frugiferum*. In Greek, of course, the god Kronos is routinely identified with time through the notorious similarity of the two words Κρόνος and Χρόνος. The Latin Saturn is likewise equated with time by the Third Vatican Mythographer (see *TMMM* 2.53), who transmits a lengthy explication of the god's iconography entirely along this line; significantly, as an allegory of the seasonal fluctuations of cold and heat that time brings, Saturn is here said to have *modo faciem draconis ... nunc rictus leoninos*. Whether or not Arnobius' monstrous god is actually the Mithraic figure, and whether or not, as Cumont claimed,[158] he was "generally" called Saturn in the Mysteries, the evidence at least suggests that the lion's head *intimates* Saturn and signals further the temporal aspects of that deity.

Another important witness which associates a lion's head with Saturn, but in a very different context, is Origen's *Contra Celsum* (6.30 f.). This time it is the planetary Saturn, and the context is the passage of souls. In a section which follows shortly on the discussion of the Mithraic *symbolon* of the seven-gated ladder (6.22), Origen reports the results of his own and Celsus' researches on the system of celestial ascent of the Gnostic sect of the Ophites. The ascent follows the commonplace Gnostic pattern of passage through the planetary spheres guarded by archons of strange appearance and arcane nomenclature. Of these, the "first and seventh" is Ialdabaoth; he is "lion-like," and he is related to Saturn: φασὶ δὲ τῷ λεοντοειδεῖ ἄρχοντι συμπαθεῖν ἄστρον τὸν Φαίνοντα (6.31; cf. 30 "Celsus said that the first is formed in the shape of a lion"). The significance of this text is emphasized by both U. Bianchi and J. R. Hinnells in their discussions of the lion-headed figure in the Mysteries;[159] for not only does it warrant the conclusion that the Mithraic figure too controls the passage of souls, but it also illustrates a shared concern with the celestial journey as a mode of salvation. Of course, Mithraic ascent is not Ophite ascent. For one thing, as is pointed out, the Mithraic planets, as tutelary gods of the grades, lack altogether that aura of malevolence and of

---

[158] Cumont (*TMMM* 1.77) seems to me to overstate his case here. Of his four pieces of evidence (n. 6 to p. 77) on which "we can affirm with certainty" that the lion-headed figure was generally called Saturn, only the Arnobius passage says anything at all about the figure's nomenclature, whether general or occasional, in the cult. That the figure should be Saturn *qua* time was of course very important to Cumont, since it was a step in establishing the equation with the Iranian god of infinite time, Zurvān.

[159] Bianchi, "Mithraism and Gnosticism," *Mithraic Studies*, 457-465, at 463 ff.; Hinnells (above, n. 111), 358-360.

power and will to frustrate which the archons of the Gnostic system always seem to carry to a greater or lesser degree. But the similarities at least suggest that the Mithraic figure, *qua* leonine Saturn, might represent in some way the Mysteries' processes of celestial journeying and control over those processes. The figure's attribute of keys (see above) would here come into play, signifying the opening or closing of the gates of the spheres; likewise, of course, the cosmic settings of the Barberini and Ottaviano Zeno figures as the arena of the soul's journeying, and especially the planetary altars as the spheres of passage.

The Arnobius and Celsus/Origen passages are familiar coin in discussions of the Mithraic snake-encircled figure. A third piece of evidence that links a lion's head to Saturn has remained out of circulation, even though its relevance was noted by Cumont himself — though in a non-Mithraic context and many years after *Textes et monuments*. It is an item in the iconography of Jupiter Heliopolitanus, specifically in the images of the planets which, with other symbols, adorn the long sheath-like garment which covers the god's trunk and legs. Quite apart from the detail concerning Saturn, the iconography of these statues is of interest to us here, first because, as E. Will pointed out,[160] they and similar statues of universal deities such as Artemis of Ephesus and Aphrodite of Aphrodisias, richly adorned with cosmic symbols and in stiff hieratic poses with legs locked close together, are probably the models and antecedents for the Mithraic figure; and secondly because the ordering of the images of the planets upon them, in the form of busts of the gods, shows some signs of thought and sophistication. In this astrological concern, expressed on the monuments, the Syrian cult of Jupiter Heliopolitanus is demonstrably our closest approximation to the Mysteries of Mithras.

In an article "Le Jupiter héliopolitain et les divinités des planètes," Cumont established for a statue from the collection of Charles Sursock (now in the Louvre) that the busts down the figure's front are indeed the planetary deities and that they are arranged as follows:[161]

Sun	Moon
Mars	Mercury
Jupiter	Venus (bust of Juno)
Saturn	

---

[160] *Le relief cultuel gréco-romain* (Paris 1955), 192.

[161] *Syria* 2 (1921), 40-46. The statue is no. 232 in Y. Hajjar, *La triade d'Héliopolis-Baalbek* (2 vols, EPRO 59, Leiden 1977). Hajjar endorses Cumont's reading of the planetary orders: see Vol. 1, pp. 278-281. A particularly interesting statue, though not immediately relevant to our study here, is Hajjar no. 233 from the Clercq collection (Cumont, pp. 42 f.). The seven planetary gods are arranged in the horoscopic order (see above, p. 7), while on the back of the statue are added five other busts to complete a set of twelve tutelary deities of the signs or months.

The key discoveries were first that the armed bust is Mars, not Athena-Minerva,[162] and secondly that the bust which is indeed that of Juno stands for the planet Venus in accordance with a widely current alternative system of planetary nomenclature and identification;[163] Juno is shown in order to form a pair with Jupiter, thus echoing the pair of Sun and Moon at the top. The handling of Juno-Venus demonstrates both a nice sense of design and a subtlety and complexity of thought reminiscent, alone among the cults, of Mithraism. Equally subtle is the option, inherent in the design, of reading the planetary sequence in either of two ways. As Cumont demonstrated (p. 43), the obvious order is from left to right pair by pair from the top: this yields the days of the week from Sunday through to Saturday. But a different order can be generated by reading in columns from top to bottom, starting on the right, and ending with the singleton, Saturn: Moon, Mercury, Venus; Sun, Mars, Jupiter; Saturn. This latter is the "Chaldean" order by distance from the earth outwards. Thus, at a more abstract level, space and time are both represented on the robe of this universal sovereign god.

Beneath the bust of Saturn on the Sursock figure is a large lion's mask. This would perhaps be unremarkable — for there might be no intended connection between the two — were it not for the arrangement on two other statues of Jupiter Heliopolitanus, one from Marseille and the other from Beirut.[164] In both there are six paired busts as on the Sursock figure (though not quite in the same combinations).[165] But there is no seventh below, no bust of Saturn;

---

[162] As R. Dussaud, "Jupiter Héliopolitain: Bronze de la collection Charles Sursock," *Syria* 1 (1920), 3-15.

[163] Cumont (above, n. 161), 41, nn. 1 and 2.

[164] Hajjar (above, n. 161), nos. 284 and 209 respectively. Cumont (above, n. 161) in fact deals only with the Marseille monument (no. 284).

[165] The precise orders are problematic. The Marseille statue (Hajjar, no. 284), on which some of the busts are rather worn, probably had the following order:

Sun	Moon
Venus	Mercury
Mars	Jupiter
Saturn	
(as lion's mask)	

The Beirut figure (Hajjar no. 209) poses an extra difficulty, not because of the loss of almost all of the busts of Sun and Moon, but because two of the remaining four are virtually identical. The two are bearded males, and by elimination one of them must be Jupiter and the other, despite its appearance, Mercury. Hajjar (*ad mon.*) sees the upper of the two as Jupiter and the lower as Mercury. I would reverse those identifications and postulate the following sequence for the set:

Sun	Moon
Mercury	Venus
Jupiter	Mars
Saturn	
(as lion's mask)	

in its place we find only the lion's mask. The conclusion that Cumont advances (admittedly, with some reservations) is that the lion's mask is the substitute and symbol of the planetary Saturn.[166] In a note (3 to p. 45), he relates this datum to the lion-headed "Kronos mithriaque."

The lion's head completes this brief survey of the iconography of the snake-encircled figure. That iconography is far from simple. However, its associations are primarily — indeed, almost entirely — celestial: with the heavens and the heavenly bodies, with the zodiac and the planets, with the path and journeyings of the Sun and Moon, with time and the seasons measured out thereby. Within this arena it speaks of power and control — in particular, and esoterically, of control over the celestial ascent and passage of the soul which was the pilgrimage of the initiate and the proper business of the Mysteries (see above, n. 90). In giving expression to these matters and processes, the figure relates to three specific gods, each of whom is also a planet (this common quality is *not* trivial or fortuitous): the Sun, Jupiter and Saturn. Each of these gods, these planetary powers, might be thought of as the figure's "person" — not, I hasten to say, in the sense of Christian theology, but in the more literal

---

In this way, both monuments would follow the same pattern and principle of organization, though with an inversion of right and left in the second and third pairs:

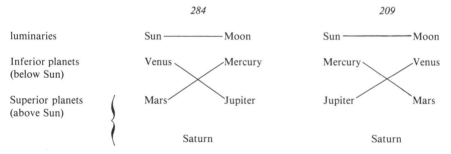

	284	*209*
luminaries	Sun ——— Moon	Sun ——— Moon
Inferior planets (below Sun)	Venus Mercury	Mercury Venus
Superior planets (above Sun)	Mars Jupiter	Jupiter Mars
	Saturn	Saturn

The bars link week-day pairs: Sunday-Monday, Tuesday-Wednesday, Thursday-Friday. Again, both dimensions of time and space are implicated in the arrangement, the latter in the grouping together of the planets below the Sun (i.e. closer to earth) in the second level and of those above the Sun (i.e. more distant) in the third and fourth. An added similarity between the two monuments is that both have herms (with *kalathos* on 284; also on the lost part of 209?) extending upwards between the pairs of gods.

[166] See also R. Mouterde, "L'astrologie a Héliopolis-Ba'albek: *Jupiter Heliopolitanus Rex* et *Regulus*," *Bull. du Musée de Beyrouth* 13 (1956), 7-21, at 13 f. Hajjar (above, n. 161) is cautious in his interpretations. He accepts that the lion's mask is Saturn on the Marseille and Beirut statues (nos. 284 and 209) where there are only six busts, but elsewhere (see esp. Vol. 1, pp. 293-295) prefers to see it as symbol of the Sun or of Athena-Allāt. Two other monuments should finally be mentioned. The first, a fragmentary statue from Byblos (Hajjar, no. 222) shows (l. to r.) Jupiter, Saturn and Venus in one compartment and a large lion's mask centrally in the compartment below (i.e. underneath Saturn). The second, a lost statue once in Graz (Hajjar, no. 313) promoted Saturn over the Sun and Moon by placing his bust centrally over theirs (the other planets perhaps being represented by rossettes below — with two for Venus as both evening and morning star).

and original ancient sense of a mask under which a role is played. It may be, however, that the metaphor ought to be inverted; for the figure itself might also be thought of as the mask under which the three gods perform. Perhaps it is helpful to think both of the gods as identities of the figure and of the figure as an identity of the gods. The latter point of view would correct too positive a conception of some final and single reality behind the snake-encircled figure that the former might engender. Conversely, the former avoids mistaking the figure for a mere portmanteau which the latter perhaps suggests.

We are now ready to return to the set of planetary altars graced by the two snake-encircled figures of the Ottaviano Zeno monument. First, one must determine the *direction* of the sequence: left to right or right to left? This is of some importance because, depending on the choice, the altar of the wingless figure will be either first or last. Perhaps, though, one should not press the necessity of choice too hard. It may be that the wingless figure is intended to be *both* first *and* last, to preside as "first and seventh," like the leonine and Saturnine archon of *Contra Celsum* 6.31, over both beginning and end.

In this interpretative game one both can and should eat one's cake and have it. Multivalence is of the essence. So one allows the possibility not only of reading the order in both directions but also of finding a privileged direction. The privileged direction, I suggest, is from right to left, which assigns the wingless figure to the last altar. What signals this direction is not so much the enhancement of meaning for altars and figures if one reads them in this way — that is consequence rather than impetus — as the relative positions of Sol and Luna at each end. Now the Moon in the Mysteries, as elsewhere, is the inferior of the Sun: in the tauroctony, the lunar bull is overcome by the solar Mithras. Moreover, in all our planetary orders the Moon is "below" or "earlier than" the Sun: in the "Chaldean" order the Moon is closer to the earth; in the grade order Perses precedes Heliodromus; in the order of the days of the week one moves in time from Monday through to Sunday. Thus, I think, any viewer, and particularly a Mithraic viewer, when confronted with a row of seven altars, manifestly planetary, with Sol at one end and Luna at the other, would proceed from Luna's end towards Sol. Here, indeed, may lurk a reason for a peculiarity, already noted (above, p. 47), in Sol's iconography on the Ottaviano Zeno monument. Normally, when the luminaries are shown with chariots and teams, both drive in profile to the right. But the Ottaviano Zeno Sol is shown frontally. The effect — and intention? — is to deny that Sol is the starting point of a movement left to right along the sequence of altars. Finally, of course, one remembers that right to left is the direction on the only monument on which the planetary sequence above a tauroctony is made explicit, namely the Bologna relief with its row of busts.[167]

---

[167] Vermaseren ([above, n. 49], 52 f.) rightly cites this precedent.

The row of altars on the Ottaviano Zeno monument falls, as it were, mid-way in degree of determinateness between, for example, the planetary busts of the Bologna relief and the seven empty and identical arches of the floor mosaic of the Sette Sfere Mithraeum. At Sette Sfere (see above, p. 14) one could place in imagination — or mime — any planet in any "sphere." The only limitation would be that the sequences so generated should have significance and some contact with an accepted reality. On the Bologna relief, at the other extreme, there is one definite and explicit sequence, although, as we saw, that sequence has more than one connotation. The Ottaviano Zeno sequence is partly open and partly closed. On the one hand, the seven altars are identical, hence indeterminate; on the other, the snake-encircled figures, related to the first and fourth (i.e. central) altars, prescribe certain limitations: one could not, for example, without absurdity postulate an order in which either of the two privileged altars stood for Venus. What the Ottaviano Zeno arrangement allows — and herein lies the subtlety and genius of the composition — is the possibility of a limited number of different sequences in which the two figures and their altars would shift their identities, though always within the range of significances that the iconography and ideology of the snake-encircled figure permit.

Significantly, the Ottaviano Zeno relief is not the only monument in which we find, in a row of seven, the central and far left items privileged. *CIMRM* 399/406, we have already noted (above, p. 14), is a marble block, of some size, from the Mithraeum of S. Silvestro in Capite, in which a row of seven niches has been carved for the display, it is generally and rightly assumed, of images of the planetary gods. Of the niches, the first on the left is distinguished by a smaller interior niche on its rear wall and the fourth and central by an interior arch.[168] By moving the images of the planets to different arrangements within the niches, one could achieve physically the various significant sequences with the same emphasis on the central and final planets that can be effected imaginatively on the upper register of the Ottaviano Zeno relief by assigning different identities to the seven altars. Both monuments function, as it were, as abacus frames for a sort of arcane celestial computation. It bears repeating that *CIMRM* 399/406 was dedicated by the grandson of the mithraeum's founder whom he describes — the phrase is notorious — as *caelo devotus et astris*.

Three different planetary sequences fit the framework of the Ottaviano Zeno altars (likewise, I suggest, the S. Silvestro niches). None is in any sense logically prior to either of the two others. However, it best fits the explication to start with the esoteric sequence, the order of the grades of the Mysteries:

---

[168] D. Gallo (above, n. 34), figs. 3 and 4; p. 234 quotes Henzen's description.

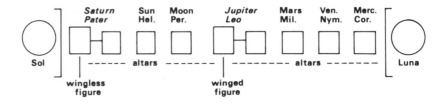

Here, the snake-encircled figures and their altars stand for Jupiter and the lions in the centre and Saturn and the Fathers on the left. Both Jupiter and Saturn, as we saw above in exploring the iconography, are "meanings" of the snake-encircled figure. Moreover, it is understandable that emphasis should be placed on the Fathers and the Lions, on the Fathers of course as the senior and ruling grade, on the Lions as the first of the true "participants" (μετέχοντες: see Porph. *De abst.* 4.16) and as the pivotal grade with the function, vital to the cult's economy, of fiery purification (see above, p. 61). It is no accident that these two grades are by far the most frequently attested epigraphically.[169] In the most grade-conscious of all mithraea, Sa. Prisca, it is the Lions who predominate numerically and in the attention paid to their processions on the frescos.[170]

With the grade identities assigned to the altars and the two figures, we meet something of a paradox. The central figure is winged, the figure on the left wingless. And yet, in the Mysteries, it is the *first* grade (corresponding to the altar on the right) that is "winged," being the grade of the Ravens. The same is true of the *last* grade, i.e. the grade which corresponds to the altar on the left and the *wingless* figure; for as Porphyry tells us, the Fathers were also called "eagles" and "hawks."[171] Furthermore, while the central figure bears a sceptre and the figure on the left does not, it is the Father, not the Lion, whose symbol on the Felicissimus mosaic is the sceptre — for the very good reason that it is the Father, not the Lion, who wields final authority in the cult.

Here, I think, the ideology of the grades is in tension with a tenet of Mithraic theology. On the present reading, the figure on the left is Saturn and the figure in the centre Jupiter. Now it was a commonplace of myth and theology in antiquity that the governance of the world had passed in "pre-history" from Kronos-Saturn to Zeus-Jupiter. The "fact" figures in the

---

[169] See the indices to *CIMRM* (I, p. 352; II, p. 427).

[170] It might be argued that the Heliodromus is the most important after the Pater. And so, in a sense, he is; for it is he who shares the banquet with the Pater, as Sol with Mithras. Nevertheless, in the actual remains of the cult he is a somewhat shadowy and ill-attested figure (like the Perses). It is the Lions who, after the Fathers, enjoy the prominence.

[171] I accept Gordon's reading and brilliant vindication of the essential soundness of Porphyry's information here: *art. cit.* (above, n. 6), 65-67.

Mithraic cycle,[172] for we find on the monuments a subsidiary scene (admittedly, not a common one) in which authority passes from Saturn to Jupiter not by violence and usurpation, as it does in the standard mythic versions, but in orderly fashion and by solemn contract. Thus, on the great Neuenheim relief (*CIMRM* 1283, scene 9) we see the veiled Saturn passing the thunderbolt to Jupiter over an altar; and Jupiter in his other hand bears the sceptre, which presumably he has also just received. Thus, it was Mithraic doctrine that Jupiter has acquired what Saturn has surrendered. And so we find them in the two figures on the upper register of the Ottaviano Zeno monument. Perhaps there is even a lesson here for the ideology of the grades: that the Father to some degree renounces his authority (as, in a different way, the Miles renounces his crown: Tertullian *De cor.* 15), transferring it to the Lion as his agent and executive. This, however, is frankly speculative; for no source or monument, unless it be this one, intimates any such surrender on the Father's part. Yet it is plausible, since the Father, after all, is by definition of rank he who is completing or has completed his terrestrial and celestial voyage, his journey though the grades and through the planets. Of all the initiates, then, he is the least in need of the props and encumbrances of office.[173]

In the diagram above, the Sol and Luna of the Ottaviano Zeno register are bracketted off because they play no part in the initial assignment of the planets to altars in the grade order. They are not juxtaposed with their altars as are the figures of "Saturn" and "Jupiter." However, once the grade order has been read into the sequence of altars, Sol and Luna too can be related in a significant way. They are the other two planets which, together with Saturn and Jupiter, preside over the four senior grades, the true "Metechontes" (see above) of the Mysteries. On this reading, then, the Ottaviano Zeno register presents the figures corresponding to all four of these senior tutelary powers — and only to those four. Again, the matter is best expressed in a structural diagram in which each of the luminaries is brought inwards to its proper altar:

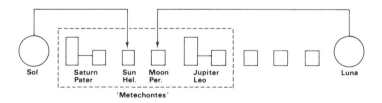

---

[172] For the career and significance of the Mithraic Saturn, see, most recently, M. J. Vermaseren (above, n. 64), 69-74.

[173] The theme of *transference* is stronly present in the Mysteries. The transference of authority between Saturn and Jupiter is but a type of this idea which we find more usually expressed in the relationship between Sol and Mithras, especially in the common scenes of the *iunctio dextrarum* and the commissioning of the kneeling Sol by Mithras.

The second sequence in which the altars of the Ottaviano Zeno monument may be read is that of order by distance from the earth (the "Chaldean" order):

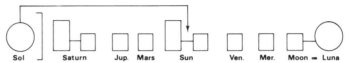

Here, the figure on the left with its altar, as before, stands for Saturn; but the figure in the middle has become the Sun, the planet which from its central position rules the cosmos and orchestrates its movements (see above, p. 6). We note that in this sequence Luna on the right is juxtaposed with her altar. Sol, of course, is not. But here, perhaps, is another reason for the unusual — on Mithraic monuments — frontal presentation of Sol and his team. The pose is manifestly that appropriate to a central element in a composition, intimating that Sol, at least on this reading, really is "in the centre."

Our first mode of reading the sequence of altars, by order of the grades, was esoteric to the Mysteries. The second mode, the "Chaldean" order, was entirely public. The third mode is mixed, basically a public order, but with significant esoteric extensions. It is the week-day order starting (on the right, of course) with the Moon or Monday; it is also, as we saw from the Bologna relief (above, pp. 22 ff.) where it is fixed explicitly in the row of busts, the order of the second decans of the signs of the zodiac from Taurus to Scorpius.

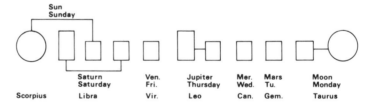

It is this order that Vermaseren rightly reads into the row of altars on the precedent of the Bologna relief (see above, n. 167). It equates the winged figure with Jupiter and the wingless with Saturn,[174] as did the grade order (our first option above). And it involves both Sol and Luna directly in the reading (hence neither is bracketed off in the diagram). It does, however, introduce a complication.[175] The wingless figure is no longer related to the altar im-

---

[174] "Aussi on serait tenté d'interpréter ce personnage central comme étant l'Eternité, soit le *Caelus aeternus* mis à place de Iupiter. L'autre figure, à gauche, serait alors la figure qui ne regne plus, Saturne." Vermaseren's equation of the Jupiter figure here with Caelus is supported, as he demonstrates, by *CIMRM* 327/328, a relief of the Capitoline Triad, arguably from the same mithraeum as the Ottaviano Zeno relief, on which Jupiter is called "Optimus Maximus Caelus Aeternus."

[175] Not taken into account by Vermaseren (above, n. 167). The other limitation in Vermaseren's treatment is of course that the multivalence of different planetary orders is not considered.

mediately to his left (i.e. the altar on the extreme left of the row). Rather, Sol and the wingless figure, as Sun and Saturn, are related *in tandem* to the two left-hand altars, Sol to the final altar which thus represents the planet of the Sun and the wingless figure to the penultimate which represents the planet of Saturn. But if that were so, why was not the wingless figure placed *between* the final and penultimate altars and related by pose to the latter? The answer of course is that in both of the other two sequences it is the final altar which is the planet Saturn. It is those two sequences which have determined the placement of the wingless figure, while for the third sequence the neighbouring figure of Sol permits a shift of relationship to the following: Sol: wingless figure :: Sun : Saturn :: final altar : penultimate altar. In all three sequences, then, the wingless and sceptreless figure, though not related to the same altar, stands for the same god and planet — Saturn. This, I believe, finally explains why he is as he is in relation to the figure who is winged and sceptred. Saturn in the Mysteries, as in the theology of the culture at large, is the god who has renounced.

The reading of the register according to the week-day order gives significance to the penultimate as well as to the final and central altars. A diagram summarizing the identities of the altars in all three orders and including the penultimate altar as also privileged is here instructive:

altar no. (from r.)	7	6	5	4	3	2	1
grade order	*Sat.*	Sun	Moon	*Jup.*	Mars	Venus	Merc.
Chaldean order	*Sat.*	Jup.	Mars	*Sun*	Venus	Merc.	Moon
week-day order	Sun	*Sat.*	Ven.	*Jup.*	Merc.	Mars.	Moon

One notes that in all three orders it is the three divine "identities" of the snake-encircled figure that fall to the privileged altars — only those identities and only to those altars. The diagram further suggests in the meanings of the final and penultimate altars some mystery of interchange between Saturn and the Sun, a mystery we shall try to probe when we return to the enigma, posed towards the beginning of this study (above, p. 7), of why a solar cult promoted Saturn over the Sun as tutelary power of its senior grade.[176]

On the Bologna relief, it was argued (above, pp. 22 ff.) that the arrangement of the planetary busts in the week-day order from the Moon (right) to the Sun (left) also intimates the signs of the zodiac from Taurus (r.) to Scor-

---

[176] Also intimated, by the central box of the diagram, is a mystery of interchange between Jupiter and the Sun. It is this mystery that, following a suggestion of R. L. Gordon ([above, n. 107], 241), I believe is alluded to in the famous Phaethon scene from the Dieburg Mithraeum (*CIMRM* 1247B). Phaethon is the descriptive name of the planet Jupiter, and the Dieburg relief shows the mythic Phaethon receiving the solar horses from a Helios whose iconography is rather that of Zeus.

pius (l.), since the same gods in the same order preside over the central (i.e. second) decans of those signs. The point of the allusion is that the elements of the bull-killing scene below, read celestially as constellations, all belong to the area of the heavens defined by that arc of the zodiac. The key to this interpretation, we noted, is the small symbols of a bull's head below Luna on the right and a scorpion below Sol on the left; the boundary signs of Taurus and Scorpius are thus explicit beneath the gods that rule their respective central decans. The same interpretation can be applied to the Ottaviano Zeno monument. The altars, read in our third mode, intimate not only the planetary gods in their week-day order from Monday to Sunday but also, through their presidency of the central decans in the same order, the sequence of the seven signs of the zodiac from Taurus to Scorpius. What is particularly appropriate is that the Ottaviano Zeno monument is also one of that very limited group of tauroctonies with the small subsidiary symbols of bull's head and scorpion to the right and left.[177] It too, then, makes explicit a part of what is intimated. Furthermore, unusually for an Italian monument, a lion is found in the field of the main scene. Thus, another of the signs of the zodiac signified by the altars — by the central one, in fact — has its overt counterpart in the scene below. Finally, and most remarkably, in addition to the principal scorpion and displacing it from the bull's genitals, the main scene has a crab — an element found in no other tauroctorny, but one that is entirely appropriate here as designating yet another of the signs alluded to in the altar sequence, that of Cancer.[178]

The upper register of the Ottaviano Zeno monument proves to be a work of great subtlety and power. In its seemingly haphazard array of components we find a flexible yet precise matrix for the generation of significant planetary orders — orders which depend on, and in turn promote reflection on, tenets of the cult's cosmology, theology, and even — since the journeyings of souls and the passage of the grades are implicated — its soteriology. Deliberately, I leave aside at this stage the application of our various orders to the altar sequence of the Barberini fresco. That is best left to a final section — and a final mystery.[179]

---

[177] See above, pp. 25 ff. with the *caveat* in n. 50. Note also the possibility—not a very likely one, in my opinion — that the upper register of the Ottaviano Zeno monument may not originally have belonged to the main scene with which the drawings associate it (see above, n. 95).

[178] The detail, which might have been doubted in the drawings, is confirmed in the recovered main stone. For those of us who take the celestial correspondences seriously, it was utterly predictable that sooner or later a crab would turn up on a tauroctony!

[179] It will be noted that no place in the interpretations has been given to the "water miracle" scene which — probably — closed the Ottaviano Zeno register at its left end (see above, pp. 46 f.). A suggestion as to its significance — its *celestial* significance, for the scene is studded with stars — will be made at the apposite place in the next section.

VIII

In addition to the various monuments, some straightforward and some enigmatic, there is one very important piece of literary evidence on planetary orders in the Mysteries. That of course is Origen *Contra Celsum* 6.22. In the context of a discussion of celestial ascent, Origen quotes Celsus (slightingly, as an example of the latter's gratuitous displays of learning) on a certain Mithraic *symbolon*:

> αἰνίττεται ταῦτα καὶ ὁ Περσῶν λόγος καὶ ἡ τοῦ Μίθρου τελετὴ .... ἔστι γάρ τι ἐν αὐτῇ σύμβολον τῶν δύο τῶν ἐν οὐρανῷ περιόδων τῆς τε ἀπλανοῦς καὶ τῆς εἰς τοὺς πλανήτας αὖ νενεμημένης, καὶ τῆς δι' αὐτῶν τῆς ψυχῆς διεξόδου. τοιόνδε τὸ σύμβολον· κλίμαξ ἑπτάπυλος, ἐπὶ δὲ αὐτῇ ὀγδόη.

"These things [i.e. celestial ascent] are intimated in the doctrine of the Persians and their Mysteries of Mithras. They have a symbol of the two celestial revolutions, that of the fixed stars and that assigned to the planets, and of the road of the soul through and out of them [i.e. the revolutions]. The symbol is this: a seven-gated ladder with an eighth at the top." The quotation then lists the metals of which each gate is made: the first is of lead, the second of tin, the third of bronze, the fourth of iron, the fifth of an alloy used in coinage (κεραστοῦ νομίσματος), the sixth of silver, and the seventh of gold. Next, the planet of each gate is given, together with an explication of the appropriateness of the metal. The logic is apparently still that of the Mithraists: "they make the first Saturn's, indicating by lead the star's slowness," etc. The order is as follows:

gate no.	metal	planet
1	lead	Saturn
2	tin	Venus
3	bronze	Jupiter
4	iron	Mercury
5	mixed	Mars
6	silver	Moon
7	gold	Sun

Here the quotation ends, though Origen further tells us that Celsus used the symbolism of nomenclature (διὰ συμβόλων ἐν τοῖς ὀνόμασι) to explain the given planetary order, and in addition certain "musical theories" (μυσικοὺς λόγους). Whether either of the last two modes of explication is Mithraic is an open question, for Origen's language is vague (perhaps deliberately so). I propose, then, to leave them out of account. In any case, even if Mithraic, there is nothing in the preserved remains of the Mysteries to which we might relate them.

This testimony tells us, or appears to tell us, that the Mysteries had a doctrine of the soul's "journey through and out of" (διέξοδος)[180] the heavens — to be precise, through the seven spheres of the planets, in a particular sequence, and the sphere of the fixed stars; and that this doctrine was encapsulated in a symbol of a "seven-gated ladder with an eighth gate on top." I say "appears to tell us" because the existence of the doctrine and the force of the symbol have both been denied, and the testimony of Celsus has been diverted into other meanings. Whether or not this passage of the *Contra Celsum* can be read at face value is absolutely crucial for our understanding both of the Mysteries' soteriology on the one hand and of their planetary lore on the other.[181] If, as I believe and shall argue, it can be so read, then we find in the Mysteries a theory of the individual soul's celestial escape (*diexodos*) in which precise planetary ordering plays a part; if not, then other matters altogether must underlie the testimony.

The *onus probandi*, it seems to me, must lie with those who would question Celsus' testimony. Why should we disbelieve him, why should we *not* take his information, at least in its main outlines, at face value? At first sight, it appears neither an absurd nor a contradictory thing to say of the Mysteries; it is not self-evidently erroneous. It fits with what Porphyry (*De antro* 6) tells us was the business of the Mysteries: "it is by leading the *mystes* through the descent and return of souls that the Persians initiate him" (οὕτω καὶ Πέρσαι τὴν εἰς κάτω κάθοδον τῶν ψυχῶν καὶ πάλιν ἔξοδον μυσταγωγοῦντες τελοῦσι τὸν μύστην). And the grade structure, we now know with complete certainty from the evidence of the Felicissimus and Sa. Prisca Mithraea (above, pp. 1 f.), was in some sense a road through the planets. Why, then, should a Mithraic symbol of a ladder "of seven gates plus an eighth" *not* intimate, as Celsus tells us it does, "the route of the soul through and out of the two celestial revolutions"?

The testimony is of course not without its difficulties, and I begin with

---

[180] I translate with deliberate literalness. On the word in context, see R. Turcan, *Mithras Platonicus* (above, n. 73), 48 f.; also R. Merkelbach, *Mithras* (above, n. 4), 236. Merkelbach (235-244) properly emphasizes the centrality to Mithraism of the soul's celestial ascent. On the topic in general, see esp. W. Bousset, "Die Himmelsreise der Seele" (above, n. 12; rp. Darmstadt 1971); P. Capelle, *De luna, stellis, lacteo orbe animarum sedibus* (above, n. 12); Th. Hopfner, *Griechisch-Ägyptischer Offenbarungszauber* Bd. 1 (Stud. z. Palaeographie u. Papyruskunde 21, ed. C. Wessely) 1921 (rp. 1974), 69-78 (149-167); A. B. Cook, *Zeus* (Cambridge 1925) 2.36-45; F. Cumont, *Recherches sur le symbolisme funéraire des Romains* (Paris 1942); C. Colpe, "Die Himmelsreise der Seele innerhalb u. ausserhalb der Gnosis," in U. Bianchi (ed.), *The Origins of Gnosticism* (Leiden 1967), 429-445; J. Flamant, "Sotériologie et systèmes planétaires" (above, n. 7); I. P. Culianu, "L' 'ascension de l'âme' dans les mystères et hors des mystères" (above, n. 12); *id.*, *Psychanodia I* (above, n. 12).

[181] The issue is well appreciated by I. P. Culianu in his review of *Mysteria Mithrae*: *Aevum* 55 (1981), 169a-172b, at 170a-b.

these, although in fact it is not any problem arising from the text itself and its literal interpretation that finally accounts for the suspicion in which it is held. First — and least worrying — is the fact that archaeology has revealed no extant counterpart to Celsus' ladder, although in form — if not precisely in content and in planetary order — the Felicissimus pavement is uncannily similar: a succession of seven rectangular compartments with planetary symbols, etc., extending ladder-like up the length of the aisle with an eighth compartment at the end with crater, twigs, and the dedication. The absence of an exact counterpart, however, proves nothing: the *symbolon* with its elaborate series of metals may have existed only notionally or in written or pictorial form; or, since we have only a tithe of the cult's physical apparatus, exemplars may still lurk undiscovered, and many, no doubt, would have perished or have been destroyed.[182]

A more serious difficulty is the order in which the planets figure. This order, as is obvious, is that of the days of the week, but in reverse, from Saturday through to Sunday. The problem here is threefold. First, although the week-day order, as we have seen, is definitely attested within the Mysteries (i.e. on the Bologna relief and the Brigetio plate: above, pp. 17 f.), nowhere do we find this particular exemplification of it. If it really is the order in which souls pass through the realms of the planets, we might expect it to occur somewhere on the monuments in preference to other less vital sequences. Secondly, and as the major cause of concern, a *temporal* order, that of the days of the week, is imposed on what is presented as a *spatial* journey, i.e. the passage through the celestial spheres. Why do we not find instead the "Chaldean" order or another of the variants which arranged the planets in sequence according to increasing distance from the earth? And, finally, why is this temporal order *reversed*, running from "later" to "earlier" or from "after" to "before" instead of with time's usual forward flow?

All these, however, are problems only if one assumes that Mithraic doctrine, in its blending of "science" and soteriology, was necessarily simple and straightforward; that it will have offered a single readily comprehensible account of the celestial voyage (if it offered anything at all in this department); and that whatever appears paradoxical or contradictory in the account as our source relays it must therefore be a mistake to be corrected. It is "wrong," so goes this logic, to impose a temporal order on a journey through space; therefore, what lies behind the testimony cannot be a celestial voyage at all.

What I hope, however, that this study so far has demonstrated is the subtlety and complexity, the variety and multivalence, in the Mysteries' use of planetary orders. From our present vantage point we should now rather

---

[182] On the ladders that we do have and on their significance, see H. Ogawa, "Mithraic Ladder Symbols and the Friedberg Crater," *Hommages Vermaseren* (above, n. 46), 854-873.

assume that the order of the *Contra Celsum* was *but one* of the orders which the Mysteries used to explore, and to conduct the *mystes* through, the mystery of the celestial voyage; that its uniqueness is therefore not a matter of concern *per se*; and that its paradoxes are deliberate and significant. Celsus has given us neither the full truth, nor a distortion of the truth, but a *partial* truth — in fact, just what we would expect to be imparted to one outside a Mystery.

We may suppose, then, that it was no mistake, but a significant mystery, that the soul should effect a primarily spatial journey in a temporal order; or rather, that this should be *one mode* in which the celestial voyage is presented to the initiate in order to illuminate, enigmatically and by paradox, a particular "fact" about that voyage: that it is *both* spatial *and* temporal. The same truth was built into the Mysteries' principal and unique planetary order, that of the grades, which, if our initial analysis was correct (above, pp. 7 ff.), deliberately blended the "Chaldean" with the week-day order. The reversal of the week-day order in the *symbolon* (from Saturday back to Sunday) perhaps intimates that same triumphing over the dimension of time which we suggested (above, pp. 10 f.) underlies the order of the planets of the three senior grades: Perses to Heliodromus to Pater = Monday to Sunday to Saturday.

The choice of the sequence's beginning and end in the *symbolon* is equally significant. It offers a fresh variant in which the principal planets, Saturn and the Sun, stand in a new relationship to each other. In the grade order (1) the two planets are last and penultimate; in the "Chaldean" order (2) they are last and central; in the week-day order of the Bologna relief (3 — as in the third mode of reading the altar sequence of the Ottaviano Zeno monument) they are penultimate and last; here in the inverted week-day sequence of the *symbolon* of the *Contra Celsum* (4) they are first and last: [183]

Order no. (above)	Planet no.			←			
	7	6	5	4	3	2	1
1	Sat.	Sun	x	x	x	x	x
2	Sat.	x	x	Sun	x	x	x
3	Sun.	Sat.	x	x	x	x	x
4	Sun	x	x	x	x	x	Sat.

[183] I retain in the diagram the right to left progress that we find visually in the planetary sequences of the Ottaviano Zeno monument. Orders 1-3 in the diagram are of course our three modes of reading the row of altars in the upper register of that monument (above, pp. 67 ff.). The order of the *Contra Celsum* (no. 4) cannot plausibly be read into the Ottaviano Zeno altar sequence; for that sequence, through the identification of the winged and sceptred figure with the central altar, stresses the planet in the middle, and the planet in the middle in Celsus' *symbolon* is only Mercury, a mere satellite of the Sun and the tutelary power of the lowest grade (though he is, one might counter, both a winged god and a psychopomp!).

From the diagram above one may immediately appreciate the significance of the new order: it adds a sequence in which Saturn is first to those in which he is last, and so teaches that Saturn, like the Ophite lion-headed archon of the first and seventh planetary gates (*Contra Celsum* 6.30 f.: above, pp. 62 f.), stands at and controls the beginning as well as the end of the celestial journey. Finally, we have already met within the Mysteries a sequence which, like that of the *symbolon*, places Saturn at the bottom and the Moon and the Sun together at the top. It is the Housesteads birth-scene (see above, pp. 35 ff.) where the zodiacal houses of the luminaries stand at the summit of the composition and the houses of Saturn at the base:

Contra Celsum 6.22		*Housesteads*		
	Sun	house of Moon	house of Sun	
	Moon			
	x	x	x	houses of
other	x	x	x	other
planets	x	x	x	planets
	x	x	x	
	Saturn	house of Sat.	house of Sat.	
		(noctural)	(diurnal)	

Arguably, the Housesteads birth-scene also had to do with the descent and ascent of souls (above, p. 41). Thus, for all its uniqueness within the Mysteries, the planetary sequence of the *Contra Celsum* demonstrably complements the other attested orders. Taught as part of the truth, or as one view thereof, it would enrich the Mysteries' doctrine of celestial ascent. Only if mistaken for a summary of the complete doctrine does it fail or mislead.

There is another mistaken assumption that has distorted our understanding of the meaning of the *symbolon*. It is often stated, and it is virtually always implied, that the *diexodos* of the soul, whether a genuine element of Mithraic doctrine or a hypothetical matter which the Mysteries did not in fact teach, is to be understood as taking place *after death*.[184] Cumont certainly held that view, for he coupled the ascent with a theory that the soul in passing back through the planetary spheres divested itself of the qualities and encumbrances of its mortal life — a theory which R. Turcan has rightly demonstrated is entirely unattested in the Mysteries.[185] Turcan himself, although, as we shall see, he rejects the superficial reading of the *symbolon* as

---

[184] See also above, n. 133.

[185] Cumont, *The Mysteries of Mithra*, trans. T. J. McCormack (London 1903, rp. New York 1956), 144 f.; Turcan, "Salut mithriaque et sotériologie neoplatonicienne," *La soteriologia dei culti* ... (see above, n. 7), 173-191, at 181 ff.: "Aucun texte, aucun temoignage écrit ou figuré n'autorise l'application au mithriacisme de la doctrine des qualités ou passions afférentes aux sphères planétaires (qualités ou passions assimilées aux 'tuniques' de l'âme)" (p. 182 f.). On the theory, which is Neoplatonic and Gnostic, see, most conveniently, Culianu, *Psychanodia* (above, n. 12), Ch. 7.

a journey through celestial space, nevertheless places his most recent discussion of it squarely within the context of *posthumous* salvation: "Reste le problème posé *par les modalités posthumes* [my italics] de ce salut [i.e. Mithraic salvation]." "On admet couramment — et j'ai moi-même admis naguère — que c'était le 'symbole' de l'itinéraire sidéral des âmes après la mort. Je n'en crois plus rien."[186] What is rejected here by Turcan is not the posthumous element but the element of the voyage, not "après la mort" but "l'itinéraire sidéral."

And yet "après la mort" should never have entered the discussion. Celsus does not specify it, and our other evidence implies that the Mysteries effected the celestial voyage *in this life*, in the here and now. It is within the Mithraic cave that the *mystes* is initiated by being led through "the descent and return of souls" (Porph. *De antro* 6: above, p. 74), and it is precisely for that purpose that the mithraeum is organized as an "image of the cosmos" equipped with symbols of its "climates and elements" (*ibid.*).[187] And the grades themselves lead one "through" the planets. The point is so nearly made by R. Merkelbach in his survey of the cult's cosmology: "In den sieben Weihen wurde also der Weg der Seele durch die Planetensphären auf Erden vorweggenommen."[188] True — except that the "soul's way" is not "anticipated on earth;" in the Mysteries, it is *realized* here on earth.

It is easy to see, however, why the celestial journey of the *symbolon* should have been understood as posthumous. First, it is a paradox, almost an absurdity, that a person should voyage through the heavens while still on earth, that he should pass through the planets while his two feet are yet firmly placed on the ground — albeit the ground of a cosmic model. So paradoxical is it that critics, who look in the Mysteries for "rational" solutions, simply fail to entertain it, although all the evidence points that way, and import instead an alien and unfounded — yet seductively logical — assumption that the journey

---

[186] *Art. cit.* (preceding note), 181, 182.

[187] τῶν κοσμικῶν στοιχείων καὶ κλιμάτων. *Stoicheia* I take to mean *inter alia* the planets. See LSJ *s.v.* II.5. Cf. Lucius' description of his ecstatic voyage during his Isiac initiation (Apuleius *Met.* 11.23): ... *per omnia vectus* elementa *remeavi*. *Klimata*, astronomically, are latitudes; hence, in the symbolic context of the mithraeum, stations from north to south — perhaps for the miming of a progress from the gate of descent in Cancer at the universe's far north through to the gate of ascent in Capricorn at the south: see Porph. *De antro* 21 f. "... there are two extremities in the heavens, the winter tropic than which there is nothing more southerly and the summer tropic than which there is nothing more northerly. The summer tropic is in Cancer, the winter in Capricorn. ... the gate through which souls descend is Cancer and that through which they ascend is Capricorn. Cancer is northerly and suited for descent; Capricorn is southerly and suited for ascent."

[188] *Art. cit.* (above, n. 121), 250; but note the next sentence: "*nach dem Tod* [my italics] sollte die Seele durch die veränderlichen Kreisläufe der Planeten hindurch zur Fixsternsphäre aufsteigen." "Veränderlichen" I take to be an allusion to the fact that the grade order of the planets is not the same as the order of the *symbolon* of the *Contra Celsum*. Merkelbach repeats this description of the doctrine of celestial ascent *verbatim* in his *Mithras* ([above, n. 4], 244).

cannot be undertaken until the soul has been liberated from the body in death: *first* one dies, *then* one goes to heaven. Yet, as Richard Gordon has reminded us and has demonstrated so cogently for the Mysteries,[189] paradox and "absurdity" are the very stuff of religions: one expects them to eat their cake and have it, to get to heaven while still on earth.

Secondly, the great literary versions of the celestial voyage are all posthumous in the sense that they imply that the heavens or the further reaches of the cosmos belong properly to those who are finished with this life (or have not yet entered it) and that the living, who report these matters, are interlopers in a realm which is not yet theirs. So it is in Plato's "Myth of Er" in the *Republic*, so also in the *Somnium Scipionis* of Cicero's *De Republica*, and so too in the myths of Plutarch's *De genio Socratis* and *De sera numinis vindicta*.[190] It is assumed, then, unthinkingly that the same must apply to the Mysteries. But the assumption is a dangerous one for the actual religious practice. No shaman waits until death to make his ecstatic journeys; and the heavenly voyage of the "*Mithrasliturgie*" is undertaken within the life of the adept — indeed, he tells us precisely when and by what *earthly* means it is to be accomplished.[191]

That the *symbolon* of the *Contra Celsum* is widely supposed to refer to something other than a literal voyage of the soul through the heavens, I suggest, is very largely an accident of the history of scholarship — and of the order of discovery of certain monuments. The trend-setting figure, as so often, is Franz Cumont; and the influential work is his long article of 1931 on Mithraic (and other) eschatology, "La fin du monde selon les mages occidentaux."[192] Cumont allowed that at least at one level the *symbolon* carried within the Mysteries its superficial and literal meaning of the soul's journey; it intimated, indeed, "un des dogmes capitaux d'une religion de salut" (p. 47). But he had noticed, and was rightly concerned about, the week-day order of the planets. Could this have to do with some originally *temporal* and perhaps very different process? Now when Cumont was writing "La fin du monde ..." the spectacular Dieburg Relief with its unique Phaethon scene (*CIMRM* 1247B) had recently been discovered. Cumont believed that this monument confirmed for the Mysteries a Magusaean eschatology such as is found as a myth in literary form in Dio *Or.* 36 (39-57). His attention was therefore fo-

---

[189] Art. cit. (above, n. 6), *passim* but esp. p. 39.

[190] One could add Plutarch's *De facie quae in orbe lunae apparet*, which also deals with the celestial afterlife, except that, unlike the others, it has no cosmic traveller, no Er to make the journey and report back.

[191] A. Dieterich, *Eine Mithrasliturgie* (3rd ed., Leipzig and Berlin 1923, rp. Stuttgart 1966); M. W. Meyer, The "*Mithras Liturgy*" (Missoula, Montana, 1976). For the *praxis* of the ascent, i.e. instructions as to when and how, see Meyer, pp. 20 ff.

[192] *Revue de l'Histoire des Religions* 103, 29-96. The section on the *Contra Celsum symbolon* is pp. 44-62.

cused on time and the end of time, and the *symbolon* of the *Contra Celsum* was fitted within this eschatological frame. He postulated, accordingly, that the week-day order of the *symbolon* conceals a succession of seven world ages ruled by the planets in a different guise as *chronocrators*, culminating in the rule of the Sun who is both Apollo and Mithras.[193] Then follows a universal conflagration, and a final age, "le règne du 'Ciel éternel' qu'on identifiait avec le temps infini" (p. 62), to which corresponds the eighth gate added to the seven in the *symbolon*. The real meaning of the *symbolon*, its "signification première et véritable" (p. 47), thus proves to be a Magusaean doctrine, blended with astrology, about the course of history and the end of time.

What had *not* been discovered when Cumont wrote "La fin du monde ..." was the Felicissimus pavement; nor of course had the Sa. Prisca dipinti. It is these two monuments that within the Mysteries tie the planets in sequence to the grades and thus to the life of the initiates. Manifestly, they relate much more closely, despite the discrepancy in actual planetary order, to the *symbolon* of the *Contra Celsum* than do eschatological monuments or texts.[194] Had they been extant and had the Dieburg monument *not* been extant, Cumont's fullest account of the *symbolon* might well, I suggest, have been very different.

Cumont's interpretation has recently been reinforced by R. Turcan whose influential *Mithras Platonicus* (above, n. 73) devotes a chapter (pp. 44-61) to Celsus and the *symbolon*. Turcan follows Cumont in his understanding of the primary meaning of the *symbolon* — that it denotes a series of world ages leading to a great renewal — and of its largely Iranian origin and ethos. Where Turcan parts company with Cumont is over the latter's belief that the *symbolon* still carried for the initiate its literal and superficial meaning of a voyage of the soul through space in a process of personal — and posthumous — salvation. For Turcan the temporal process of the Great Year, which the Mithraic ladder symbolizes, is the destiny both of souls and of the world: "Ce que signifiait en revanche le 'symbole' mithriaque, c'était la rénovation intégrale du monde et corrélativement des âmes, 'l'apocatastase', au terme de la Grande Année sidérale" (p. 54). Or, as he puts it more recently,[195] "les âmes doivent passer successivement par les temps d'une grande semaine sidérale qui correspond à l'accomplissement d'un cycle cosmique ..." What then of the soul's voyage through celestial space about which Celsus appears to be talking? For Turcan this is a misunderstanding or a distortion of what the

---

[193] Apollo: to accommodate the testimony of Nigidius Figulus *ap.* Servius *ad Ecl.* 4.10 (see Cumont, *id.* 44 f.).

[194] One might add that it is a hypothesis, not a self-evident fact, (a) that the Mithraic relief of Phaethon (Dieburg) is eschatological and (b) that the eschatological material of the Dio myth and the Nigidius Figulus *testimonium* (preceding note) have anything to do with Mithraism.

[195] "Salut mithriaque ..." (above, n. 185), 182.

Mithraists in fact believed. It is part and parcel of a systematic reinterpretation of Mithraic evidence by Neopythagoreans and Neoplatonists to suit their own cosmologies, their own theories of the soul, and their own soteriologies. That is the general thesis of *Mithras Platonicus*, and Celsus' version of the ladder symbol is but one — though a very important one — of the items in Turcan's dossier of Neoplatonic distortions of Mithraic doctrine.

It is not my intention here to confront the theories of Cumont and Turcan head-on. Since they clearly have very wide ramifications, to challenge them on all counts would involve a disproportionate space in a study of quite limited compass and would carry us too far afield in arguments remote from Mithraic planetary doctrine. It is my concern rather to plead for leaving a place for the literal reading of Celsus' testimony and for the interpretation of the *symbolon* at face value as signifying the ascent of the soul through the planets and the sphere of the fixed stars. This I hope I have accomplished earlier in this section. Let it be conceded here — though I am sceptical — that a doctrine of world ages is also intimated, even that it derives in part from Iranian originals.[196] What does require attention, however, is Turcan's view that the testimony is contaminated at source. It was argued above that the testimony, read at face value, fits well with what Porphyry says in the *De antro* about the role of celestial descent and ascent in the Mysteries. That, however, on Turcan's theory is a draught from the same poisoned well, since Porphyry is within the same Neoplatonic tradition. So if Turcan is correct about the systematic Platonizing of the evidence, neither the words of Porphyry nor those of Celsus are to be trusted as meaning quite what they say about the Mysteries. In my view, however, Turcan, while demonstrating amply that the various testimonies are consistent with Neoplatonism, does not prove that they are also inconsistent with the Mysteries. He thus fails to counter the perfectly plausible argument that in much of their respective cosmologies, anthropologies and soteriologies Neopythagoreanism and Neoplatonism on the one side and the Mysteries of Mithras on the other *converged*.[197] There is no

---

[196] For a full and, I believe, effective critique of Cumont's Mithraic eschatology, see R. L. Gordon (above, n. 107), 233-240, esp. 237 ff. In sum, it is a precarious structure (see above, n. 194): what is Mithraic in it is dubiously eschatological, and what is certainly eschatological is dubiously Mithraic. In "La fin du monde ..." (above, n. 192), emphasis was rightly placed on the metals associated with the planetary gates: these are not the standard associations of Graeco-Roman astrology, but Cumont failed to prove that they were therefore somehow derived from Iranian sources. For a brief, but not very telling, critique of Turcan, see Culianu *Psychanodia* (above, n. 12), 52 f.: Turcan's reconstruction is not invalidated merely by the fact that it is not directly attested.

[197] It is not even necessary to determine who influenced whom: in the formulation of such theories, one may simple suppose a like doctrinal response, by philosophers on the one side and a practiced religion on the other, within the same culture and in response to the same stimuli and concerns.

reason why the doctrine on the soul's celestial voyage should not have been *both* Neoplatonic *and* Mithraic.[198]

The credibility of Celsus' account of the *symbolon* is somewhat enhanced by an often overlooked detail in the account itself. All along, we have been treating the *symbolon* as if its first meaning is — or is not — the *diexodos* of souls. But that is not precisely what Celsus says. The ladder, with its seven gates plus an eighth, he says, is a symbol "of the two celestial revolutions (περιόδων), that of the fixed stars and that assigned to the planets, and of the road of the soul through and out of them [i.e. the revolutions]."[199] In other words, the first and most literal significance of the ladder of seven and one is the two celestial revolutions, and it is through that primary denotation that the ladder signifies the passage of souls. Celsus' account is thus rather more elaborate and round-about than might seem necessary for the logic of his explication. Why the emphasis at the start on the two revolutions? Why not simply say that the Mithraists had a symbol of the soul's passage through the spheres of the planets and of the fixed stars? The answer, I suggest, is that Celsus is here faithfully recording the actual explication of the Mysteries, and he does so even though the detail is irrelevant to the flow of his own argument. Now we know both from the monuments and from the texts that the Mysteries were in fact much concerned with the two celestial revolutions. The detail of Celsus' testimony can thus be confirmed independently. And if this detail is genuine, then the second, that the symbol intimates the passage of souls, is likely to be genuine also, for the two merge together seamlessly as the two steps in a single explication — which, we may be sure, is that of the Mysteries.

It remains to confirm the Mysteries' interest in the two celestial revolutions. The distinction between these two "periods" is fundamental in ancient thought. For it involves not merely different spatial locations (the planets within, and the sphere of the fixed stars at the boundary of, the universe) and different speeds of revolution (the sphere of the fixed stars daily, the planets each in its proper period, from the Moon's month to Saturn's 29 years), but also the basic polarities of unity and multiplicity (the "Same" and the "Different" of the *Timaeus*: above, n. 58) and of the two directions of motion (westwards and to the right for the sphere of the stars and for the universe in general, eastwards and to the left for the planets: above, p. 29; also n. 37). It is this last distinction, as I have demonstrated elsewhere,[200] that is faithfully

---

[198] In a complicated argument that starts in the chapter on Celsus but culminates in the following chapter on the *De antro*, Turcan seeks to show that the theory of gates of descent and ascent in Cancer and Capricorn cannot have been Mithraic. In a future study — for it requires some considerable length — I shall try to demonstrate quite the contrary: that the theory is integral to the Mysteries and intimated in their iconography, notably — and this we shall see in the present study — in the Barberini fresco. See above, n. 93.

[199] Clearly, αὐτῶν refers to περιόδων, not πλανήτας: Turcan (above, n. 73), 49 f.

[200] *Art. cit.* (above, n. 37), 9 ff.

replicated in the celestial orientation of the cult icon of the tauroctony. The two revolutions are further exemplified in certain of the monuments examined in the present study. In the Barberini fresco, of the two arcs spanning the scene, the upper, that of the altars, represents the spheres of the planets, the lower that of the zodiac, the sphere of the fixed stars.[201] It is significant that the snake-encircled figure in the middle links the two, for the globe on which he stands interrupts the zodiac while his head masks — or is — the central altar. His stance thus perhaps intimates the "fact," which is the primary truth of Celsus' *symbolon*, that both orders are implicated in the celestial ascent of the soul. In the Bologna relief we saw (above, pp. 21 ff., esp. 29 f.) that the zodiac was intimated, through the link of the decans, in the planetary sequence itself. The directions of the two revolutions also figure in this monument, as in others. The sequence of planetary deities, arranged in the weekday order, runs from right to left; and the same is true, we argued, of the sequences of planetary altars on the Ottaviano Zeno monument, in whichever of the three modes it is read. By analogy with the Bologna relief it is also true of those many undifferentiated sets of seven altars which span the monuments between Luna (Monday) on the right and Sol (Sunday) on the left (above, p. 30). This movement from right to left alludes, I suggest, to the leftwards or eastwards motion proper to the revolution of the planets (above, n. 37). In the scene of the tauroctony beneath, however, the movement, in this case the visual impetus, is from left to right: the bull is moving that way when it is brought down, and Mithras appears from the cloak streaming behind him to be rushing in that direction too.[202] This, I believe, given the icon's alignment, intimates the universe's primary rightwards or westwards motion, the revolution of the sphere of the fixed stars in which all celestial bodies participate. In that Mithras is the Sun and the bull in some measure the Moon, their directions in the icon replicate that primary motion. These intimations are explicitly reinforced by the directions of Sol and Luna above the scene; for with remarkably few exceptions, when shown with quadriga and biga respectively, they drive their teams to the right and to the west.[203] That this *daily* motion of the luminaries is indeed intended (rather than the annual and monthly) is revealed in the fact that Sol is shown rising as in the morning while Luna is descending as if setting.

---

[201] The scheme of the fresco is here "unscientific," for in reality the sphere of the fixed stars lies *above* the spheres of the planets.

[202] The fact that the mantle is the vault of heaven itself (see its rendering in, e.g., the Barberini and Marino frescos and the sculptures *CIMRM* 245 and 310) emphasizes that Mithras' apparent impetus is celestial motion in a given direction.

[203] Beck (above, n. 37), 9. See above, p. 47, on frontal representations of Sol's quadriga, of which the Ottaviano Zeno monument contains one of the (at most) three Mithraic examples in this location (i.e. upper l. of tauroctony).

The Mysteries' concern with the two celestial revolutions was a part of a much larger interest in opposition and polarity, principles which we find explored in the monuments most obviously in the persons of the two torch-bearers.[204] But that interest also crops up in the texts — if, that is, one may accept as ultimately drawn from Mithraic sources certain data from Porphyry's *De antro*. In ch. 29 of that work, Porphyry is explicating allegorically the two entrances, one for mortals and the other for immortals, of Homer's cave in *Od*. 13.103-112:

> "Since nature arose out of diversity, the ancients everywhere made that which has a twofold entrance her symbol. For the progression (πορεία) is either through the intelligible or through the sensible; and when it is through the sensible, *it is either through the sphere of the fixed stars or through the sphere of the planets*; and again it is made either by a mortal or immortal road. There is a cardinal point above the earth, and another below it, one to the east, and one to the west. There are regions to the left and right, there is night and day. And so there is a harmony of tension in opposition *and it shoots from the bowstring through opposites (καὶ διὰ τοῦτο παλίντονος ἡ ἁρμονία καὶ τοξεύει διὰ τῶν ἐναντίων).*" (trans. of Arethusa edn.)

There are several reasons for treating this text as derived (at least in part) from the Mysteries, quite apart from the general nature of the *De antro*, a work in which, I hazard the conjecture, matters explicitly attributed to the Mysteries by Porphyry or his sources are merely the tip of a pervasive Mithraic iceberg. First, there are the resonances of the oppositions found, as we have just seen, within the icon of the Mysteries: east and west, left and right, night and day. Secondly, there is the uncanny echo of the *symbolon* of the *Contra Celsum*, "either through the sphere of the fixed stars or through the sphere of the planets." Here, surely, is the generalized doctrine (or an aspect of it) intimated by the ladder symbol. Thirdly, there are the overtones of technical astrology so strikingly characteristic of the Mysteries, evident here in the inclusion of the "cardinal points" (κέντρα).[205] But lastly and most compellingly, there is the final item, which breaks with the pairs of natural and cosmic polarities and substitutes instead a single metaphor: the bow's tension in harmony, which "shoots through opposites." The metaphor signals, I suggest, a *symbolon*, and if so it is not difficult to detect its visual counterpart within the Mysteries of Mithras: the scene of Mithras as archer.[206]

---

[204] See my "Cautes and Cautopates ..." (above, n. 37); also of importance for understanding the *reversal* of polarities in these two figures is R. L. Gordon's "The Sacred Geography of a Mithraeum ..." (above, n. 29), 127-130.

[205] For definitions of the *kentra*, see Bouché-Leclercq (above, n. 7), 257 ff., Neugebauer and Van Hoesen (above, n. 16), 3.

[206] If so, the original understood or expressed subject of τοξεύει for the *symbolon* within the Mysteries would have been Mithras himself, not an abstract ἁρμονία. Ultimately, of course, the saying is derived from Heraclitus fr. 51 DK.

And so we return to the upper register of the Ottaviano Zeno monument. That work, it seems most probable (above, pp. 46 f.), closed on the left with the scene of Mithras shooting at the rock before which a second figure kneels. The kneeling figure, which was the only one extant when the drawing for the intaglio was made, is surrounded by stars,[207] an element which does not occur in other examples of this scene and which suggests a special emphasis here on its celestial dimensions. The postulated meaning should now be clear: the scene functions as a symbol of the two revolutions in which those celestial bodies represented by all the other components of the register participate — and beyond that, of the soul's *diexodos* through those two revolutions.

IX

We return now to a paradox, noted much earlier (p. 6 f.), in the planetary order peculiar to the Mysteries, that of the grades. Why did a solar cult, in formulating a sequence linked to promotion up a hierarchy, put the Sun in the penultimate position rather than in the final and most senior? The same problem may be viewed from another angle, positively rather than negatively. Saturn's place at the head of the sequence was emphasized in the very structure of the order in that the two luminaries are together interposed in the sequence of the five other planets in the "Chaldean" order just below him (see above, p. 7):

> Saturn
> Sun
> Moon
> Jupiter
> Mars
> Venus
> Mercury

Why should Saturn (it seems at the Sun's expense) be so signally honoured?

Various answers may be returned. One, that Saturn is at the top because the grade of Pater which he oversees is the senior grade, while the Sun's grade (Heliodromus) is only the penultimate, would obviously be unsatisfactory, for it merely begs the question of why these solar cultists chose to assign not the Sun but Saturn to their senior rank. More telling would be Saturn's undisputed position as the furthest and "highest"[208] of the planets and that nearest to the sphere of the fixed stars. His tutelage of the highest grade in-

---

[207] Nine stars: see above, n. 101.
[208] A planet's distance from the earth is technically its "height" (ὕψος).

timates that the Pater is he who has proceeded furthest on his heavenly pilgrimage, he who is most remote from things terrestrial and closest to things celestial. Also, but by a different type of argument, one might refer to the genesis of the grade order as a conflation of the week-day and "Chaldean" orders, deliberately so structured to allude to the twin dimensions of time and space: see above, pp. 9 ff. Saturn, as the diagram there shows, stands at the head of both contributing orders, and his position in the grade order might be seen in part as stemming from the logic of that order's design.

There is, however, a more satisfactory answer than any of the above — satisfactory because it both accounts for Saturn's promotion, if one may so call it, and at the same time ameliorates the apparent demotion of the Sun. The answer invokes an equation or proposition of identity: Saturn can be set at the head and the Sun relegated to second (or penultimate) place *because Saturn is the Sun*. Therefore, where we see Saturn we also see the Sun (and vice versa): and so, arcanely and by paradox and enigma, it is still the Sun that we find at the head.

Now this identification of Saturn with the Sun is not something deduced from the known doctrine of the Mysteries or inferred from their iconography. Rather, it is a "fact" of exoteric "science," on which, I would claim, the Mysteries drew for the design and validation of their unique planetary and grade order. In ancient astrology it is widely attested — although not to the extent of being a routine commonplace known to all — that Saturn was the star of the Sun. From our perspective, the most important testimony is that of Ptolemy in the *Tetrabiblos* (2.3.64), for Ptolemy links the identification to Mithras-worship, though not explicitly to the Mysteries. Speaking of the inhabitants of the S.E. quarter of the world (including Persia and Babylonia), he says that they "worship the star of Aphrodite [i.e. the planet Venus], naming it Isis, and the star of Kronos [i.e. Saturn] as Mithras Helios." The earliest allusion to the identification is in the Platonic *Epinomis* (987C); thereafter we find it, *inter alia*, in the Eudoxus Papyrus (col. 5), Diodorus (2.30.3), Hyginus *De astron.* 2.42, 4.18, Servius (*in Aen.* 1.729), and Simplicius (*in De caelo*, p. 495.28-29 Heiberg).[209]

Why Saturn should be identified with the Sun is far from obvious.[210] What can, however, be stated with certainty is that Graeco-Roman astrology made

---

[209] Among modern authorities, see Bouché-Leclercq (above, n. 7), 93, n. 2; F. Boll, *Sphaera* (Leipzig 1903), 313, n. 3; *id.*, "Kronos-Helios," *Archiv f. Religionswiss.* 19 (1919), 342-346; F. Cumont, "Les noms des planètes et l'astrolatrie chez les Grecs," *L'Antiquité Classique* 4 (1935), 5-43, at 14, n. 2.

[210] A contributing factor may have been a perceived affinity, manifested in closely similar names, between the Greek Sun god Helios and the Semitic god El equated with Kronos-Saturn: see Bouché-Leclercq (preceding note); Boll "Kronos-Helios" (prec. note), 342 f.; A. I. Baumgarten, *The Phoenician History of Philo of Byblos: A Commentary* (EPRO 89, Leiden 1981), 180 ff.

the identification because Babylonian astrology had made it already, and the western tradition here simply drew on its older eastern relative. Diodorus explicitly attributes it to the Chaldeans, and Ptolemy, as we saw, associates it, *inter alia*, with Babylon. By itself, this would establish little, for much — perhaps most — astrological lore was attributed either to the "Chaldeans" or to the Egyptians. Our identification, however, is one of those rather rare pieces of information which is actually true of Mesopotamian astronomy. As M. Jastrow documented,[211] Šamaš, the name of the Sun, is found on certain tablets as a synonym for Lu-Bat Sag-Uš, the proper name of Saturn, and glosses on the texts point out that it is being so used. Jastrow (p. 164 f.) mentions a tablet which, to indicate that the real Sun and not Saturn is intended, speaks of "Šamaš of the day." Although the complementary phrase is not attested (as far as I can ascertain), it seems that Saturn was the Šamaš of the night, the surrogate or counterpart of the Sun in the night-time and the illuminator *par excellence* of the hours of darkness. Certainly this is how Saturn's identification with the Sun is generally understood,[212] although, as mentioned, the reason for Saturn's choice for the role rather than another planet or the Moon remains obscure. It is in this sense of the night-time Sun that Saturn's image or symbol is sometimes interpreted on the monuments of Jupiter Heliopolitanus,[213] in particular on the Donato bronze (Hajjar no. 153),[214] where the god appears in a large central compartment, below the Sun and Moon, his head emerging from a huge star-studded veil which surely represents the heavens which he rules and illuminates at night.

If, as I suggest, the doctrine of Saturn as the noctural Sun was part of the Mysteries, used eventually to sanction their peculiar planetary order, it could be argued that it was acquired at a very early stage, indeed well before the definitive formation of the Mysteries in the West. As an item of genuinely Chaldean lore, it could have been collected during that transitional phase when, on Cumont's classic reconstruction,[215] the Mithras cult passed through Babylon on its way from its Iranian cradle to its Roman maturity, acquiring at that intermediate stage its astrological teachings. Indeed, the use of the Saturn-Sun identification in Mithraism, if we accept it, would be a formidable piece of evidence supporting the hypothesis of a Babylonian stratum in Mithraic doctrine. It is not, however, compatible *only* with that hypothesis. Were it a purely Babylonian doctrine, unattested in the West, then indeed it would have to have been acquired in Babylon and would virtually confirm the

[211] "Sun and Saturn," *Revue d'Assyriologie* 7 (1909), 163-178.
[212] Thus Jastrow (preceding note), Boll "Kronos-Helios" (above, n. 209), 345, Cumont (above, n. 209).
[213] See esp. R. Mouterde (above, n. 166), 13.
[214] (above, n. 161), 1.172 ff.
[215] See esp. *TMMM* 1.72.

hypothesis of the Babylonian phase. As we have seen, however, it is also well attested in the West, even before the emergence of the Mysteries there. It is thus equally valid to suppose that the Mysteries, as in other matters, took it over from the occidental astrology of their own culture. Regardless of its ultimate Chaldean provenance, which would not in this case be known, its reputed "Chaldean" flavour would no doubt have recommended it to this self-consciously "Persian" religion. This latter is to me the more likely scenario. But whether the cult inherited the Saturn-Sun equation as something handed on from Mithras-worship in the east, or whether it was re-invented by the founding sages of the cult in the West, what matters here is that it was a "fact" of astrological science (whether Chaldean or "Chaldean") which the cult at some stage acquired from outside itself and used — if my theory is correct — to legitimize an idiosyncratic structure. As such, it fits with what we have seen to be the pattern of Mithraic doctrine where things celestial are concerned. The peculiar is never entirely arbitrary. New combinations are formed, new and esoteric truths are developed, but they are generated from, and hence validated by, the old and the accepted (if sometimes rather recherché) truths of a common science.

The identification of Saturn with the Sun enriches our reading of other planetary sequences used in the Mysteries apart from the grade order — an indication, perhaps, that it was truly present in the cult's doctrine. The progress in the *symbolon* of the *Contra Celsum* was from Saturn to the Sun. We see now that it is also from Sun to Sun — or from Saturn to Saturn, which is virtually what Celsus tells us of the sequence of the archons in the analogous Ophite ascent through the spheres (6.30 f.): the leontomorph Ialdabaoth rules both first and seventh spheres and "is in sympathy with the star Phaenōn (Saturn)." At any rate, the identification of Saturn with the Sun intimates that in the sequence of the Mithraic *symbolon* the beginning and end are in some sense the same, that one returns to the starting point, but at a higher level; thus, while overtly the metaphor of the ladder signals rectilinear progress (ascent straight up), the *symbolon* in its beginning and end also hints at the ascending spiral of the helix, which is the metaphor of that other Mithraic symbol of celestial ascent, the snake-encircled figure.

Turning next to the planetary orders behind the altars of the Ottaviano Zeno monument, we find that the Saturn-Sun identification illumines not only the grade order but also the other two modes of construing the sequence of the altars with their concomitant figures. Our second mode (p. 70) was the "Chaldean" order by planetary distance. Here, the wingless snake-encircled figure is related to the final (i.e. extreme left) altar as Saturn, the last and most distant of the planets, and the winged snake-encircled figure is related to the middle altar as the Sun, the central and ruling planet mid-way between earth and heaven. The fact that essentially the same snake-encircled figure is related to both intimates, I suggest, the astrological equation linking the two planets. The third mode of reading the altar sequence (p. 70 f.) was according to the days of the week. Here we postulated that Sol and the wingless figure relate in tandem to the final and penultimate altars as Sun and Saturn (Sunday and Saturday). The joint identifications are surely enhanced if we take into account the "fact" that the Sun and Saturn are in a sense one and the same:

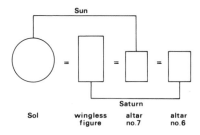

The identification of Saturn as the noctural Sun prompts some further reflections on the central bust in the planetary sequence of the Bologna relief; also on the bust at the summit of the larger Dura relief (*CIMRM* 40) which is analogous in location and form.[216] By position in the sequence, the central planetary god of the Bologna relief is Jupiter; yet, iconographically he is Serapis or Pluto, for he bears on his head the *kalathos* or *modius* which is the symbol of the lord of the underworld. The god of the Dura relief, set in the middle of the span of the zodiac and forming a triad with Sol and Luna, likewise bears the *kalathos* and is thus also to be identified with Serapis-Pluto. Yet he also wears a crown of rays and is accordingly a solar deity too. Thus we find in the same upper central location, at the heart of other celestial symbols (Sol, Luna, planets, zodiac), a god who in one instance is both Jupiter and Serapis-Pluto and in the other both the Sun and Serapis-Pluto. One seeks, in particular, to understand why the underworld associations obtrude in this context.

An answer may lie in the concept of the alternative Sun, the Sun not of daytime or the world above, but of night-time and the world below. With this Sun is naturally equated the lord of the underworld who is both Hades/Pluto and, from the Egyptian mysteries, Osiris/Serapis. "Pluto," says Porphyry (Περὶ ἀγαλμάτων fr. 7),[217] "is the Sun going beneath the earth and voyaging round the invisible world ..." It is this Sun whom Apuleius' Lucius sees — and worships, it is implied — in the mystic *katabasis* of his initiation (*Met.* 11.23): "I approached the confines of death and trod the threshold of Proserpina; borne through all the elements, I returned. At mighnight I saw the Sun gleaming

---

[216] On the two busts, see above, pp. 32 ff., 51 f., with diagrams; also n. 67 on the London and Sa. Prisca Serapis heads. On the authenticity of the Bologna bust, see Appendix.

[217] *Ap.* J. Bidez, *Vie de Porphyre* (Ghent 1913, rp. Hildesheim 1964), Appendices p. 9.

with a pure light. I approached the presence of the gods below and the gods above (*inferos ... superos*); I worshipped them close by."[218] Macrobius (*Sat.* 1.20.13-18, 21.11 f.) confirms the equation of Osiris/Serapis with the Sun; also (1.20.15) that the *kalathos* could in itself serve as a solar symbol, intimating "the height of the Sun and his power to contain, since all earthly things return to him, drawn there by the heat let loose on them." On our two Mithraic monuments, then, we may suppose that the bust at the summit who wears the *kalathos* and who is identified thereby as Pluto-Serapis is also the Sun — indeed, the rays of the Dura figure explicitly point that way — but a different and special Sun: the Sun who illumines and guides towards a world which is not that of our ordinary earthly life lit by the quotidian Sun but which is rather the under-world where "the Sun shines at midnight." This midnight Sun is Pluto or Serapis; but in the Mysteries (if our hypothesis is right) he is also, and more fundamentally, Saturn. So, in an image of remarkable density, the central bust of the Bologna sequence evokes no fewer than four deities: by position, Jupiter; by iconography, Pluto-Serapis; by the associations of the preceding, the Sun of the underworld and mystic initiation; by the esoteric equation of the nocturnal Sun, Saturn.[219]

---

[218] For the original Egyptian fusion of Osiris and the Sun god Rē, see J. Gwyn Griffith's commentary *ad loc.* (*Apuleius of Madauros: The Isis-Book* [EPRO 39, Leiden 1975], 303 f.).

[219] It is surely a strong argument for the authenticity of this figure that no restorer of the early 19th century (or before) could possibly have grasped this rich network of equations — or would have dreamed of applying it — prior to the discovery of the complementary Dura figure: see Appendix.

It is these equations that justify *CIMRM*'s unargued identification of the Dura bust as "Saturn-Serapis." Cumont ("The Dura Mithraeum," trans. and ed. E. D. Francis, *MS* 1.151-214, at 166 f.), less happily, saw it as Baal Shamîn, "identified with the Mazdean Ahura Mazdā, lord of the sky, the Iuppiter Caelus worshipped by Mithraists even in the West." But that has more to do with pre-conceived Mithraic theology than with the actual appearance of the god which is not at all that of Baal Shamîn: see S. B. Downey, "Syrian Images of Mithras Tauroctonos," *Etudes Mithriaques* (above, n. 147), 135-149, at 142.

Related to the concept of a separate identity for the nocturnal or infernal Sun is the idea of equating different gods with the Sun at different seasons. This clearly underlies the famous oracle of Apollo of Claros (Macrobius *Sat.* 1.18.20 citing Cornelius Labeo) on the identity of Iao as supreme (ὕπατον) among the gods: "in winter Hades, at the start of spring Zeus, in summer Helios, and in autumn splendid Iao." In the season of his greatest power the sun naturally appears under his own name; significantly, at the nadir of his power he is Pluto. It is an intriguing fact, though no more than a coincidence (but an evocative one!), that all four aspects of this seasonal Sun are intimated in the two busts of the Bologna and Dura reliefs: Hades by the *kalathos*, Zeus by the position of the bust in the Bologna sequence, Helios by the Dura busts's solar rays; and as for the autumnal Iao, at Dura the bust is set among the signs of the zodiac precisely at the autumn equinox. On the oracle, and on Labeo as the probable source of much of the Neoplatonic solar theology conveyed in the surrounding chapters (1.17-23) of the *Saturnalia*, see P. Mastrandrea, *Un neoplatonico latino: Cornelio Labeone* (EPRO 77, Leiden 1979), 159 ff.

Professor Vermaseren has alerted me to another monument which might intimate the equation of Saturn and the Sun within the Mysteries. It is *CIMRM* 494 from Sa. Prisca (see Vermaseren and Van Essen [above, n. 2], 346 with Pl. 80), a plaque with a bust of Sol — the rays are cut out, probably for illumination from behind — made of *lead*. Lead of course is Saturn's metal, as in the *symbolon* of *Contra Celsum* 6.22 (above, p. 73).

X

Saturn will also be the final concern of this last section — Saturn and, once again, the snake-encircled figure. But the route there is indirect, and we must return first to the fresco of the Barberini Mithraeum (see diagram, fig. 5).

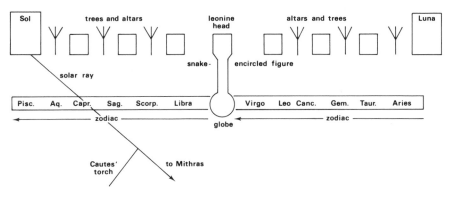

Fig. 5. *Linear schematization of the arcs of the altars and of the zodiac above the tauroctony of the Barberini fresco (CIMRM 390)*

Throughout this study I have argued that the planets and the planetary sequences in the Mysteries are intimately bound up with that celestial journey which, I claim, was so central a concern of the cult and its soteriology. Now the Barberini fresco furnishes, in a detail of the composition that has — surprisingly — escaped detection, cogent proof of this celestial journey and confirmation, moreover, of the version found in Porphyry's *De antro*. The detail, however, directly concerns the zodiac of the fresco rather than its planetary altars. Nevertheless, it is highly relevant, for the zodiac and the set of planetary altars are closely linked in the composition — bound together, indeed, by the snake-encircled figure who both stands on the globe that divides the two halves of the arc of the zodiac at its summit and marks with his head the central altar of the set of seven. Moreover, as we have seen with the ladder *symbolon* of the *Contra Celsum* (above, pp. 82 ff.), planets and zodiac in Mithraism are but aspects of a single mystery. Consequently, in demonstrating the celestial voyage in one we establish it — or at least enhance its probability — for the other.

With a row of planetary gods or symbols one asks, what order? With a zodiac, however, where the sequence of signs is immutable, the initial question is, where does the sequence start? On the Housesteads birth scene (*CIMRM* 860: above, pp. 35 ff.) we saw that the unusual commencement with Aquarius was a key of sorts to the significance of the composition. In the Barberini fresco, in contrast, the sequence starts with Aries (on the right), which is completely banal and therefore non-informative.[220] A consequence of that commencement is that the globe on which the snake-encircled figure stands is set between Virgo and Libra, i.e. at the autumn equinox. But we cannot with any certainty claim that that setting was intentional or significant, for it may be no more than the inevitable result of the designer's choice to follow a routine deployment of the zodiac beginning with Aries. If, coincidentally, there is significance, it would probably lie in the fact that the equinox — actually the two equinoxes together — were considered Mithras' own cosmic setting, his "proper seat" (οἰχείαν χαθέδραν, *De antro* 24). Also, it is worth noting that according to the oracle of Apollo at Claros (see above, n. 219) autumn was the season at which the supreme god Iao, who was the Sun in summer, Zeus in spring and Hades in winter, takes on his true name and identity. Were the Barberini Mithraists perhaps playing with a similar enigma in setting their snake-encircled figure (a god who, as we have seen, also has affinities with — or is — the Sun, Zeus and Hades) at the autumn equinox? The rayed bust with *kalathos* in the Dura relief occupies the identical point in that monument's zodiac.

The point of the autumn equinox between Virgo and Libra would coincide with the summit of the zodiac arc whichever direction were followed by the sequence of signs, whether from right to left or left to right, provided only that Aries is the initial sign. The positions of all other points, however, and indeed of the signs themselves, would be affected: what would lie to the right of centre on one arrangement would lie to the left on another, and vice versa. Now the Barberini zodiac, together with one other exception, is alone among arciform Mithraic zodiacs in running from right to left.[221] It is conceivable, then, that the norm was here deliberately overridden in order to bring a particular part of the zodiac on to the side it would not usually occupy. Is there some element obviously so affected?

When the question is so posed, one's attention is immediately caught by Capricorn. It is through Capricorn that the ray extending from Sol to Mithras (a not unusual feature of the more elaborate tauroctonies, especially the frescos) pierces the arc of the zodiac. No other sign is distinguished in any way

---

[220] Aries is the initial sign on all arciform Mithraic zodiacs except those on the Housesteads birth-scene (see above) and on the soffit of the cult-niche at Dura (*CIMRM* 43: begins with Libra in lower right): *CIMRM* 40, 389, 390, 635, 1083, 1137A, 1149, 1292. It is also the usual starting point in lists, etc.; note, from within the Mysteries, the Sa. Prisca text: *primus et hic Aries astrictius ordine currit*.

[221] See preceding note for the list of monuments. The other exception (right to left) is *CIMRM* 43. It is worth noting that the Barberini Mithraeum also had a zodiac running in the other direction (left to right) over the arch of the cult-niche: traces of Pisces on the far right are preserved (described under *CIMRM* 389). The Dura Mithraeum, too, had zodiacs running in opposite directions: *CIMRM* 40 (zodiac of the larger relief — left to right) and 43 (zodiac of the soffit of the cult-niche — right to left).

whatever (except perhaps by position in the sequence — e.g. Aries as first). Is there, though, any reason why Capricorn rather than another sign should be set at this point of intersection? A positive answer may indeed be found in Mithraic doctrine.

First, however, let us look more closely at the composition. The ray from Sol to Mithras passes not only through the symbol of Capricorn but also through the tip of Cautes' torch. The torch is narrow and elongated, reduced virtually to a straight line about equal in length to the ray, which it intersects at right angles.[222] The geometry of the composition is indeed remarkable;[223] once noticed, it is clearly significant:

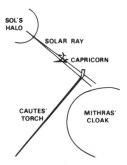

For the significance of the composition we may turn now to Porphyry and the *De antro*. Prophyry is explicating allegorically the cave with two entrances, one for men at the north end and the other for immortals (ἀθανάτων) at the south, which Homer describes in *Odyssey* 13 (102-112). For part of his account (ch. 21 ff.) Porphyry draws explicitly on the Neopythagorean Numenius of Apamea and his associate Cronius for a doctrine of the descent and return of souls into and out of earthly genesis and the material world (which the cave symbolizes) through the celestial gates of Cancer in the north and Capricorn in the south respectively. The gates, Porphyry emphasizes (24), are not in the east and west or at the equinoxes, Aries and Libra,[224] but in the north and south at the solstices, which are the directions in which Homer, for allegorical purposes, sets the entrances of his cave. Within this expository frame Porphyry next introduces (*ibid.*, probably from the same source) a doctrine that Mithras, as "creator and lord of genesis" (δημιουργὸς ... καὶ γενέσεως δεσπότης), was assigned the equinoxes as his "proper seat" (οἰκείαν καθέδραν). Clearly, the implication in context is that Mithras as the master of *both* pro-

---

[222] For this reason, I suspect, the ray is brought down to Mithras' cloak instead of to his face as, e.g., in the Marino fresco.

[223] To maintain accurate proportions, the diagram below has been traced from a photograph.

[224] Although it makes no astronomical sense, Porphyry treats the equinoxes on the one hand and east and west on the other as equivalent terms. This is done by (false) analogy with the solstices which are indeed the extreme northern and southern points of the ecliptic.

cesses, of entering this world and of leaving it, of apogenesis as well as of genesis, cannot be set at one or other of the two gates but must be positioned mid-way between them to signify that he controls both. Appended to this information on "Mithras' seat" is the further detail (*ibid.*) that Cautes is set in the south "because of the heat" (διὰ τὸ εἶναι θερμόν) and Cautopates in the north "because of the coldness of the wind" (διὰ τὸ ψυχρὸν τοῦ ἀνέμου).[225] Since cold and a cold wind are then explicitly related to genesis and heat and a hot wind to apogenesis (25), Cautes is firmly identified with the latter process and Cautopates with the former. Cautopates, in sum, is the power who has to do with descent, generated by cold, into mortality through the gate of Cancer; Cautes with ascent, generated by heat, out of mortality through the gate of Capricorn. This "fact", or at least Cautes' half of it, is what we see graphically portrayed in the composition of the Barberini fresco. The raised and burning torch of Cautes abuts onto the beam between Sol and Mithras that passes through Capricorn.[226] Just so, souls ascend under the power of Cautes, or by the power which Cautes symbolizes, and pass into apogenesis through the gate of Capricorn.

That the *solar* ray should be the path of apogenesis can likewise be confirmed from literary sources. In the *De antro* (29) the gates of souls are ascribed not only to Cancer and Capricorn but also to the Moon and the Sun, and it is "through the Sun" that souls ascend (καὶ διὰ μὲν Ἡλίου ἀνιέναι). Even more apposite is the testimony of Julian. In the *Hymn to the Mother of the Gods* (*Or.* 5, at 172) he discusses the apogenetic function of the Sun's rays: "one must believe that the anagogic rays of the Sun are proper to those hastening to be released from genesis" (172A ἔχειν οἰκείως πιστευτέον τοῖς

---

[225] The names were restored to the text in the Arethusa edition of the *De antro* (Buffalo 1969). This brilliant emendation is absolutely secure, for not only does it make sense of a corrupt text by the restoration of proper Mithraic material in a Mithraic context, but the vestiges of the names were still there in the corrupted text, cobbled into an approximation of sense by the copyists (see the apparatus *ad loc.*). The origin of the corruption is obvious: failure to comprehend two unfamiliar proper names.

[226] On one detail there appears to be a discrepancy. In Porphyry Cautes is *on Mithras' left*, but in the Barberini fresco he is on Mithras' right — although from the viewer's perspective he is *on the left of Mithras*. Porphyry and his sources probably intended right and left from Mithras' point of view, so it is more likely than not that the text and the monument are in fact in disagreement here. Two factors, however, complicate the question. First, the actual wording of the text is at this point uncertain: ἔχων, of Mithras "*having* north on the right and south on the left," is an editors' supplement to link the clauses. Secondly, the respective positions of the torchbearers on either side of the tauroctonous Mithras notoriously shift. On the Barberini fresco Cautes is on the left of the scene (Mithras' right), following the norm for Roman and Italian monuments (and, I would claim, to link him and his torch to the beam connecting Mithras with Sol). But elsewhere in the Empire Cautes is more often on the right, hence indeed on Mithras' left; and that is also almost invariably his position in a mithraeum, a separate statue or relief being set on the right-hand bench, i.e. to the left from the point of view of Mithras in the cult-niche (see R. L. Gordon [above, n. 29], 127 ff.). It is probably this latter arrangement that Porphyry's information on directions reflects.

ἀφεθῆναι τῆς γενέσεως σπεύδουσι τὰς ἀναγωγοὺς ἀκτῖνας ἡλίου). Not only is this true of physical and growing things, Julian argues, but it also applies spiritually, intellectually and morally: "since [the Sun] accomplishes this among material things through material heat, how could he not, through the invisible, entirely incorporeal, divine and pure essence situated in his rays, draw and lead up the souls of the fortunate?" (172B ὁ γὰρ ἐν τοῖς σώμασι διὰ τῆς σωματοειδοῦς θέρμης οὕτω τοῦτο ἀπεργαζόμενος πῶς οὐ διὰ τῆς ἀφανοῦς καὶ ἀσωμάτου πάντη καὶ θείας καὶ καθαρᾶς ἐν ταῖς ἀκτῖσιν ἱδρυμένης οὐσίας ἕλξει καὶ ἀνάξει τὰς εὐτυχεῖς ψυχάς;). Significantly, Julian links this anagogic power of the Sun to Capricorn, for it is then (after the winter solstice) that daylight begins to increase again. Significantly too, it is in this section that Julian throws in what is generally regarded as one of his few allusions to Mithras, intimating that the foregoing is a doctrine of the Mysteries (172D, Loeb trans.): "And if I should also touch on the secret teaching of the Mysteries in which the Chaldean, divinely frenzied, celebrated the God of the Seven Rays, that god through whom he lifts up the souls of men, I should be saying what is unintelligible (εἰ δὲ καὶ τῆς ἀρρήτου μυσταγωγίας ἀφαίμην, ἣν ὁ Χαλδαῖος περὶ τὸν ἑπτάκτινα θεὸν ἐβάκχευσεν, ἀνάγων δι' αὐτοῦ τὰς ψυχάς, ἄγνωστα ἐρῶ), yea wholly unintelligible to the common herd, but familiar to the happy theurgists. And so I will for the present be silent on that subject."[227]

Two rather important consequences stem from our analysis of the composition of this element of the Barberini fresco against the literary texts. First, we see that these features in the tauroctony are not solely or even primarily details in a work of *narrative* art. They do not tell a story; at least, that is not where their real significance lies. Rather, they are doctrinal, soteriological statements at once precise and profound. Thus, superficially, the ray linking Mithras to Sol may have to do with the latter's instruction to the former to kill the bull — so, generally, it is interpreted, although actually the mandate is an inference from the scene, not an explicitly attested "fact" of the story. More profoundly, however, — and ironically our evidence for these arcana is actually better than for the more obvious surface meaning — the ray indicates the path and the agencies by which the ascent of souls is accomplished in the Mysteries.

Secondly, if the literary evidence provides the key for interpreting the iconography, the iconography in turn validates the literary evidence and proves it germane to the Mysteries. This is currently of considerable importance, since it is precisely Porphyry's information about the gates of descent and ascent in Cancer and Capricorn that R. Turcan has forcefully rejected as non-Mithraic.[228] Yet the Barberini fresco amply proves it Mithraic.

---

[227] On the Sun's anagogic powers, see also Macr. 1.20.15 (quoted above, p. 90). Cf., too, Plutarch's doctrine, elaborated in the myths of the *De facie* and the *De genio Socratis*, that while the soul comes from and returns to the Moon, the source and final destiny of the mind is the Sun.

[228] (above, n. 73), 88 f. See above, nn. 93 and 198.

To return to the composition of the fresco, we have seen how the powers of apogenesis (Cautes, Capricorn and Sol) are grouped together on the left side and physically joined by Cautes' torch and the solar beam — linked too by the latter to Mithras. On the right of the fresco, in opposition, we find the powers of genesis, although here there is no physical bond and the significance of the arrangement is apparent only by analogy and contrast with the apogenetic side. These latter powers are Luna (for the gate of descent is also called the gate of the Moon [*De antro* 29] and the Moon "she who presides over genesis" [*id.* 18 γενέσεως προστάτιδα)], Cancer and Cautopates. Actually, the composition is yet more subtle, for the sequence of planetary altars plays a part too. One of the modes in which we can read the sequence, as on the Ottaviano Zeno monument (above, p. 70) is the "Chaldean" order by distance from earth. In this mode the altar on the extreme right, close to Luna, stands for the Moon, the nearest of the planets.[229] The altar on the extreme left will accordingly stand for Saturn, the most distant. And this too fits the balance of apogenetic against genetic powers; for Saturn also is a power of apogenesis — according to the self-same explication of the *De antro* that we have already established as thoroughly Mithraic. The setting of the gates of souls in Cancer and Capricorn is justified in Porphyry's account (21-24) by the logic of the planetary houses (see above, p. 38). Cancer is the gate of descent because the Moon, a manifestly genetic power (ch. 18) and the closest to the earth which is the arena of our mortality, has Cancer as her house. Capricorn is the gate of ascent and apogenesis because it is the house of Saturn, the most remote of the planets and the god who presides over the Roman feast of liberation, the Saturnalia, celebrated in the season of Capricorn (23): "The Romans celebrate the Saturnalia when the Sun is in Capricorn, and the slaves feast and wear the clothes of free men and everyone shares in common with everyone else. The inaugurator of the festival intimated that by this gate of heaven [i.e. Capricorn] those who are now slaves by genesis are liberated through the feast of Saturn and the house ascribed to him, ascending to life (ἀναβιωσκόμενοι) and departing into apogenesis."[230] Thus, the scheme which balances apogenesis against genesis in the Barberini fresco may be extended to include the two extreme planetary altars, not only the Moon's on the right but also Saturn's on the left:

Apogenesis	Genesis
Sol	Luna
Saturn's altar	Moon's altar
Capricorn	Cancer
Cautes	Cautopates

[229] This lunar altar is also that closest to Cancer, the astrological house of the Moon.

[230] If this logic of the Saturnalia was actually used within the Mysteries to explain the roles of Saturn and Capricorn in apogenesis, it will have been especially evocative to the slaves and freedmen who constituted a sizable element of the cult in Rome.

Let us expand our analysis of the scheme by introducing the central term at each level, to see what it is that mediates between the two processes and their powers. Doctrinally, we know from Porphyry (above) that it is Mithras set at the equinoxes. What do we find correspondingly in the central (vertical) axis of the fresco?

Now the Barberini fresco can be analysed compositionally into four horizontal levels. These are not quite the same as the four pairs shown immediately above, for Sol and Luna in the fresco are set at the same level as the planetary altars. The first and uppermost level is thus the level of the planets and of Sol and Luna. Below that comes the level of the zodiac. Third, and much the largest in terms of depth (i.e. from top to bottom), is the main part of the scene of the bull-killing action; we might call this the level of the Mithraic trio (Cautes, the tauroctonous Mithras, Cautopates). Last and at the bottom is the level of the terrestrial animals,[231] the dog, the snake and the scorpion. The third and fourth levels are not spatially differentiated as are the first two, but we shall see that there is good reason in this particular context for treating the fourth as separate from and additional to the third.

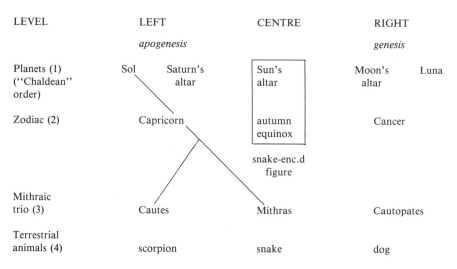

LEVEL	LEFT	CENTRE	RIGHT
	apogenesis		*genesis*
Planets (1) ("Chaldean" order)	Sol Saturn's altar	Sun's altar	Moon's altar Luna
Zodiac (2)	Capricorn	autumn equinox	Cancer
		snake-enc.d figure	
Mithraic trio (3)	Cautes	Mithras	Cautopates
Terrestrial animals (4)	scorpion	snake	dog

At the heart of the main scene (third level), his head carefully positioned on the central vertical, we find the tauroctonous Mithras set between the torch-bearers. Above, on the same central vertical and linking the first and second levels, is the snake-encircled figure. He stands, as we have already noted, on a globe set in the arc of the zodiac between Virgo and Libra at the point of the autumn equinox. The equinox — one rather than both[232] — thus figures as the

---

[231] "Terrestrial" to exclude the fourth of the attendant creatures, the raven.

[232] For a way of representing iconographically a setting at *both* equinoxes, see above, p. 40 with n. 83, on the Trier rock-birth (*CIMRM* 985).

median point at the second level. The head of the snake-encircled figure, as we have also observed, masks or is itself the central altar in the set of seven. Since the sequence in this context is that of the "Chaldean" order by distance, the central altar here stands for the Sun at the heart of the cosmos mid-way between earth and heaven. So at the first level, the planetary, it is the Sun that is at the centre. This is significant new information. We know that it is "Mithras at the equinoxes" who mediates between genesis and apogenesis. May we now infer from the altar sequence that it is essentially the *solar* Mithras who so acts? If so, since the Sun in this same scheme is an apogenetic power, the whole scheme appears to be tilted somewhat in favour of apogenesis against genesis, a bias one might in any case infer from the apogenetic beam linking Sol and Mithras through the gate of Capricorn.

On the fourth and bottom level, that of the terrestrial animals, the snake extends between the dog on the right and the scorpion on the left. Here we must demonstrate what has already been established for the other three levels, that its components have to do with the opposition of genesis and apogenesis. The scorpion is manifestly apogenetic as it seizes on the genitals of the dying bull.[233] That the dog, in contrast, is genetic, although not self-evident, is nonetheless explicitly attested. Porphyry, in the very section of the *De antro* from which so much Mithraic material has emerged, links the gate of Cancer to genesis by an argument involving the Dog Star (24): "Near Cancer is Sothis [the Egyptian term for Sirius], which the Greeks call the Dog Star. Their [sc. the Egyptians'] New Year is the rising of Sothis, *which marks the start of genesis into the world* (γενέσεως κατάρχουσα τῆς εἰς τὸν κόσμον).[234] Between the genetic dog and the apogenetic scorpion extends the snake. The whole ensemble relates to the heavens and acquires its meaning and unity therefrom; for between Sirius (or its constellation, Canis Major) and Scorpius extends Hydra. This celestial snake, writhing horizontally at the foot of the composition, echoes the ascending coils of the snake-encircled figure upright at the summit. Those coils, we saw (above, pp. 56 ff.), intimated the celestial ascent of the soul. Similarly, the snake below represents progress from genesis to apogenesis.

---

[233] The bull itself is genetic — see *De antro* 18: "souls entering genesis are 'ox-born' (βουγενεῖς)." The scorpion may also carry genetic, as well as apogenetic, associations; for its season, when the Sun is in Scorpius, is the time of *sowing*: see my "A Note on the Scorpion in the Tauroctony," *JMS* 1 (1976), 208 f. This should not be regarded as a contradiction, but rather as signifying that the two processes are complementary and interwoven.

[234] An "etymological" argument is also relevant here: κύων is not only the common noun for "dog" (and the proper noun for the Dog Star and its constellation) but also the present participle of the verb meaning "to conceive." Hippolytus (*Ref.* 4.48.10, Wendland 3.72.18 f.) ascribes this line of argument (used about the *logos* of God) to one of his heretical sects. The dog, like the scorpion, is an ambivalent symbol, for it is apogenetic too. The Dog Star is also Sirius, which means, or was taken to mean, the "scorcher" (cf. σειριάω). Its rising marks the hottest time of year (cf. our "dog days") when the Sun withers and dries out growing things, thus bringing an end to the process of genesis: see Aratus *Phaenomena*, 329-335.

In this complex allegory of genesis and apogenesis the planetary altars of the fresco are read in the "Chaldean" order with the Moon at one end, Saturn at the other, and the Sun in the centre. Let us now turn, finally, to the other two modes of reading the planetary sequences of the altars (above, pp. 67 ff., 70 ff.; cf. 31) and to the implications for the snake-encircled figure who marks the central altar. In both these orders the central figure stands for Jupiter and its associations are leonine. In the grade order, Jupiter is the tutelary planet of the middle grade, the Lions. In the order of the days of the week from Monday to Sunday, Jupiter presides over the day at the mid point, Thursday. This order, as we saw in the context of the Bologna relief (above, pp. 18 ff.), is also the order of the gods of the central decans of the signs of the zodiac in the arc from Taurus to Scorpius — the order which alludes by a system of constellation equivalents to the scene of the bull-killing below. In this more esoteric reading of the order, the central altar stands for Jupiter as the god of the central decan of Leo. This link is strengthened by the fact, also already noted (above, p. 31), that in the system which related the twelve Olympian gods to the twelve signs Jupiter is the tutelary god of the sign of Leo. Thus, both Leo and the Mithraic *Leones* are *tutela Iovis*. These leonine associations are obviously emphasized by the snake-encircled figure's head which masks or is itself the central altar. Even if that head is not actually leonine here (see above, n. 65) — although I believe it is — other examples of the figure are so routinely lion-headed that the present one could not but carry that connotation. And from the leonine we are led back to the Sun — the identity of the altar in the "Chaldean" order — since terrestrial lions are the Sun's animals and the celestial Lion is his house (above, p. 60).

I wish to suggest, as a closing "mystery," that we are led back also to Saturn. For it is in the "person" (literally and technically) of a spiralling snake, surmounted by a lion's head, and crowned with solar rays, that we meet Saturn in the sign of the Lion which is the house of the Sun. Once again, and for the last time, in exploring the arcana of the Mysteries we appeal to public "facts" — public in principle, in practice accessible at least to the learned — of contemporary astrological science. "Fact" it is that the first decan of the sign of Leo has "the form of a lion's mask with solar rays and the body entirely of a snake, upright and spiralling upwards," and that this decan is the "person" (πρόσωπον, *facies*) of Saturn, i.e. the guise under which Saturn acts in this tract of the heavens.[235] It was from this being, I suggest, that the

---

[235] ... μορφὴν δὲ [sc. ἔχει] λέοντος πρόσωπον ἀκτῖνας ἔχον ἡλιακάς, τὸ δ' ὅλον σῶμα ὄφεως σπειροειδὲς ἄνω ἀνατετραμμένον: from a Hermetic decan list, as published by C. E. Ruelle, "Hermès Trismégiste, Le livre sacré sur les décans," *Revue de Philologie* 32 (1908), 247-277, at 260. See also W. Gundel, *Neue astrologische Texte des Hermes Trismegistos*, Abhandlungen der bayerischen Akademie der Wissenschaften, Philos.-hist. Abt., N. F. Heft 12 (Munich 1936), p. 12, lines 1-4: *De prima facie Leonis. primus decanus Leonis habet faciem Saturni .... serpens est*

Mysteries ultimately drew their type of the snake-encircled, lion-headed god. Iconographically, the latter is remarkably close to the former, much closer than to any of its other postulated antecedents.[236] And the appearance of the former was already widely familiar in magical gem stones.[237] But, more important — and this would surely have been the reason for its adoption — the decan god gave "scientific" expression, and hence legitimacy, to an identification of crucial concern to the Mysteries, that between Saturn and the Sun. For the decan god is Saturn in the house of the Sun. The figure, then, encapsulates from the source of "Egyptian" learning the same truth that we have seen (preceding section) the Mysteries assert on the grounds of the "Chaldean."[238] Do we perhaps hear an echo of these things and of their application to the climax of the soul's journey in the words of Firmicus Maternus (*Math.* 5.3.22): "Saturn, positioned in the Lion, calls back to heaven and their primal origin the souls of those who have so conducted themselves, freed from innumerable restrictions"?[239]

---

magnus forma leonis habens radios solares in circuitu capitis. On this and the other decans of Leo, their forms and the varying names, see Gundel, "Leo 9," *RE* 12.2 (1925), 1973-1992, at 1989 ff. See also the table of decans in Bouché-Leclercq (above, n. 7), 232 f. On the decans in general and on the system by which they were allotted in sequence to the seven planets, see above, p. 21 f.

[236] Much closer than, for example, to the Egyptian god Bes, as in R. Pettazzoni, "The Monstrous Figure of Time in Mithraism," trans. H. J. Rose, in *Essays on the History of Religions* (Leiden 1954, rp. 1967), 180-192. The major change, obviously necessary for monumental purposes, is that a body — a human body — has been added round which the snake can spiral upwards. This also allows for the transformation of the slightly bizarre decan god into a formidable and hieratic figure on the pattern of the stiffly posed cosmic deities such as Jupiter Heliopolitanus or Artemis of Ephesus (see above, p. 63). The solar rays persist, significantly, in the Mithraic figure from Egypt, the decan god's country of origin: *CIMRM* 103 (Oxyrhynchus).

[237] See W. Drexler, "Knuphis," *Ausführliches Lexikon der gr. und röm. Mythologie* (Roscher), 2.1250-64, at 1258 ff. Note esp. the description of a gem in the British Museum, quoted on p. 1259: "the lion-headed, radiated serpent of Chnoumis, with the inscription in Hebrew, 'I am Chnoumis, the eternal Sun;' and in Greek, 'the overthrow of giants or demons;' the name Iao and another Gnostic word."

[238] There are yet further ramifications of identity. The decan god is arguably a form of the "royal star at the heart of the Lion," Regulus, the *lucida* of Leo, which, according to the scholia on Aratus (*ad* 148, p. 364 Maass), "the Chaldeans believe rules the hosts of heaven (ἄρχειν τῶν οὐρανίων)." On the basis of a dedication to Jupiter Heliopolitanus as Regulus (*I O M H Regulo*: Hajjar no. 26), R. Mouterde suggested ([above, n. 166], 14) that it is in the guise of this leonine, regal and solar star in Saturn's decan that the nocturnal Sun, which is also Saturn, is particularly manifested. Regulus, I have intimated in an earlier study (*art. cit.* [above, n. 37], n. 16), also has affinities with Mithras himself, standing to the central god of the Mysteries as the *lucidae* of Taurus and Scorpius, Aldebaran and Antares, stand to his *paredroi*, the twin torchbearers. These, however, are matters to be explored fully elsewhere — in a project whose route will lie through the heaven of the fixed stars rather than those of the planets, as here.

[239] Firmicus, of course, is talking not of the Mysteries but of astrology, in particular of the effects of the planet Saturn when in the sign Leo. "... who have so conducted themselves" translates the vague *qui sic se habuerint*; other renderings are possible.

APPENDIX

In 1976 the Museo Civico Archeologico of Bologna mounted a special exhibition of the early nineteenth-century antiquarian Pelagio Palagi. Included was the Mithraic bull-killing relief *CIMRM* 693, which has figured so prominently in the present study. In preparation for the exhibition, the relief was removed from its old setting in a wall and thoroughly cleaned. As a result of her involvement in this project, Dr. A. M. Brizzolara became convinced that the fragment in the centre of the upper rim containing four of the planetary gods (Mars, Mercury, Jupiter, Venus) was a modern restoration. She included this finding in a publication on this relief and another from the Palagi collection.[240]

Brizzolara advances a number of cogent arguments against the genuineness of the fragment. I believe, however, that there are equally cogent, though very different, considerations which militate in its favour. The purpose of this appendix is to set out the arguments on either side; also, to make explicit the consequences for my findings on the planetary gods, should the fragment not be genuine. In my study I have assumed the integrity of the whole relief, treating the fragment as authentic (though noting, wherever relevant, the other possibility), and I believe the balance of probability inclines that way. Unfortunately, any final test or judgement is now precluded, for the relief itself is no longer accessible. A few years ago it was stolen.

These are the arguments against the fragment's originality;[241] (i) that there is a difference in surface texture between the four busts on the fragment and the three on the main part: the former are rougher than the latter; (ii) that the marble is different in quality, though "chosen with care"; (iii) that the fit between the fragment and the main part is not exact; (iv) that there are markings, an A and four vertical strokes, on the reverse of the fragment which may allude to the restoration of the four deities; (v) that there are slight differences of cut and an "approximation" of detail in the four busts of the fragment; (vi) that the back of the fragment is smooth and level while that of the remainder is coarse and roughened.

Though certainly weighty, these considerations are not conclusive, either individually or in their ensemble. Obviously, the fragment is not markedly different in style or material, for this is the first time that its authenticity has been questioned. The monument is well known, especially among Mithraic

---

[240] "Due rilievi votivi della collezione Palagi," *Il Carrobbio: Rivista di Studi Bolognesi* 3 (1977), 89-102.

[241] *Id.* n. 37. The argument on the difference of the finishes of the backs of the two parts (vi) was communicated to me directly by Dr. Brizzolara.

scholars, and no one, to my knowledge, has previously doubted its integrity. This, of course, is no guarantee of the fragment's genuineness, but it does suggest that the differences which Brizzolara finds are quite subtle and should not be accepted too readily as necessarily indicative of a restoration. In the composition of the busts of the fragment, their style, iconography, and level of sophistication, I can see no real discrepancies or cause for doubt. The care in the matching of marbles which Brizzolara acknowledges permits one to wonder if the two pieces might not after all be one and the same. The remaining discrepancies can be accounted for by plausible hypotheses on different weathering of the two pieces, different initial treatment after discovery, and special preparation of the fragment for re-attachment and mounting. The relief's history is entirely unknown. If it was broken in late antiquity (e.g. when discarded, or in the destruction of its mithraeum, or in the shrine's collapse after abandonment), then the two parts could well have lain for centuries in such a configuration as to age and weather very differently. It is conceivable that after discovery the two pieces might have parted company for a time and the tiny, cameo-like upper fragment might have been re-worked for some separate setting. These, of course, are conjectures, and perhaps one would not even entertain them were it not that other factors compel one to consider the contrary view that the fragment is original.

The case for the genuineness of the fragment rests on the person of Jupiter who occupies the centre of the planetary sequence. Paradoxically, as we have seen (above, pp. 32 ff.), the figure is Jupiter only by definition of position. In iconography he is another god altogether: Serapis. Consider, then, the strangeness of the restoration — if that was what took place. The restorer has cleverly divined that what was missing was four planetary busts to complement the extant three and that the requisite order of presentation was that of the days of the week. Superficially, this may sound an easy deduction to make: three planets and a lacuna surely imply the other four. But in this context it is far from obvious. Two of the extant busts are those of the Sun and Moon serving as the usual Sol and Luna of a tauroctony, while the third, Saturn's, has no iconographic traits which unambiguously signal that god and planet. The restoration, then, if restoration it is, is so far from being straightforward and inevitable that one might wonder if it is even the *correct* restoration — a problem we must in due course address. But be that as it may, the restorer has chosen the neat but by no means obvious supplement of the planetary gods. He then, we must suppose, deliberately undermines that supplement by presenting in place of one of the four requisite planets a different god altogether. Of course, in the context of the finished set we can see that Serapis is intended to be Jupiter-Serapis, but this does not really answer the question. For while it is understandable that an original designer might wish to make the extra statement, it is not really plausible that a restorer should.

There are no data in the remainder of the monument that point that way nor, to my knowledge, any external models that would call for a Serapis in place of Jupiter in a planetary set. Why was the restorer not content with his brilliant supplement? Why the addition of what seems a mere *jeu d'esprit* whose effect is to blunt rather than to enhance the elegance of the restoration?

Now, in fact, the appearance of Serapis on a Mithraic monument, especially in the given position in the upper centre immediately above the bull-killing god, is highly apposite. But the crux of the matter is that no restorer of the early nineteenth century (or before) could possibly have known this. For the discoveries which establish its appropriateness were not made until long afterwards. The Serapis heads from mithraea (*CIMRM* 479 Sa. Prisca, 783 Mérida, 818 London)[242] have all come to light in the present century; likewise the syncretistic Greek dedication to Zeus-Helios-Sarapis-Mithras from the Mithraeum of the Baths of Caracalla (*CIMRM* 463). But the most significant monument is the larger of the tauroctonies (*CIMRM* 40) from Dura, where the mithraeum was unearthed in 1934. This relief carries a bust of Serapis in precisely the same position as on the Bologna relief. The Dura Serapis is likewise placed at the centre and culminating point of a celestial arc, though at Dura the set is that of the zodiac rather than the planets. The only other difference is that the Dura Serapis is rayed; his primary associations are thus with the Sun, whereas on the Bologna relief they were with Jupiter through position in a planetary sequence. The Dura relief, I suggest, together with the other evidence validates the Bologna relief. It reveals that there existed a Mithraic Serapis with the complex theological ramifications which we have explored at some length in the present study (above, pp. 33 f. [with nn. 67 and 68], 51 f., 89 f.) and it confirms an iconography for the setting of this figure in a certain context in the bull-killing scene. It is surely the more reasonable hypothesis that the original Mithraic designer of the Bologna relief incorporated the figure from knowledge of it and its associations than that a restorer hit on it by accident, with no awareness of its significance or appropriateness, and in plain contradiction of the apparent logic of his restoration. To judge from the remainder of the relief,[243] its Mithraic designer was precisely the sort of bold, imaginative and subtle exploiter of symbols to expand the scheme of the planetary gods by the conversion of Jupiter to Serapis. But he would do so only under the warrant which we find expressed also in the Dura relief. The hypothetical restorer could not have known that warrant. His Serapis would therefore be a lucky but inane fluke. Such things do happen, but alternative explanations are preferable. In default of the sort of conclusive

---

[242] On the Sa. Prisca and London heads and their possible settings, see above, n. 67.

[243] See above, pp. 19 ff., and note esp. the use of the torchbearers' additional symbols, the bull's head and scorpion; also n. 145, on the substitution of a winged putto for Sol and Mithras in the ascending chariot.

material proof which the disappearance of the monument has unfortunately rendered impossible, I maintain the working hypothesis that the bust of Serapis must have been part of the original design, that the fragment is therefore genuine and the entire relief authentic.

The one scenario for the restoration tentatively advanced by Brizzolara proves on closer inspection to be unlikely in the extreme. Brizzolara rightly draws attention to a drawing by Palagi of an ancient graffito calendar discovered in 1812 on a wall in a Christian chapel in the Baths of Titus.[244] At the top of the calendar are the busts of the seven planetary gods in a row. Brizzolara suggests that it may have been this design that gave Palagi the idea for the proper restoration of his relief.[245] It is no real objection to this hypothesis that the planets on the calendar run in the opposite direction and from a different starting point in the sequence,[246] though the fact ought to have been noted. What is decisive, in my view, is the calendar's Jupiter. Apart from the left shoulder and two strokes above it, the figure had been obliterated when Palagi made his drawing. If that were all, it would tell heavily in favour of the restoration of the Bologna relief with the calendar as model, for it would mean that Palagi would have been free to reconstruct his Jupiter ad *libidinem* — as Serapis with *kalathos* if he so wished. But it is not all. Palagi obligingly appended a note: "Lacerazione fatta nello scavo. Qui stava l'imagine di Giove, e i due tratti superiori alla spalla dovevano indicare i fulmini." The fact that it takes the eye of faith to discern the thunderbolts in the two lines is not of concern. What matters is that Palagi saw them there. Since he did, it follows that he cannot have used the calendar as warrant to restore the planets of the Bologna relief with a Jupiter bearing Serapis' iconography in place of the Thunderer's own.

It remains to consider the consequences for the present study should the fragment with the four planetary gods after all be a restoration. In the first place, the restoration might have been carried out with knowledge of the original. One may suppose that damage which destroyed the affected portion beyond repair or re-attachment was done *after* the monument's discovery and that the restorer did his work from a description, a drawing or memory of what had been in the original. But in that case, since our concern is with the composition, content and iconography of the relief, not with its artistic execution or with its originality *per se*, the restoration would be the exact equivalent of the original and would pose no problems for our treatment of the relief in the present study. Actually, the hypothesis has much to commend it, for it would reconcile the discrepancies of execution which Brizzolara finds with the

---

[244] (above, n. 240), 98 with fig. 10.
[245] *Id.* 100.
[246] From left to right, starting with Saturn.

knowledge of Mithraic arcana which the iconography reveals. The restorer would have known what to represent not because he had plumbed those arcana ahead of time or hit on them by a fortunate accident, but simply because he knew or was told or was shown in a drawing what the damaged original had contained and how it was composed.

If, however, the restoration was done without knowledge of the original, then one cannot assume that the original Jupiter would have had the iconography of Serapis. Though a Serapis, as we have seen, is highly appropriate there, the simpler hypothesis that Jupiter would have appeared in his own guise is probably the more likely. If that is so, then those parts of this study which build on Jupiter's identity as Serapis are to be modified or discounted (pp. 32 ff., 51f., 89 f.). Fortunately, none is central to my main arguments or theories.

Finally, we must assure ourselves of something more fundamental: that the restoration, if such it was (and if it was in fact executed without knowledge of the original), was the correct and inevitable one. In other words, is it certain that the four planetary gods, Mars, Mercury, Jupiter, Venus (in that order, righ to left) must have occupied the lacuna caused by the fragment's loss? Brizzolara assumes so without argument, and R. Merkelbach[247] states as much though likewise without argument. They are right, but the solution is not so obvious and automatic that it can be left without comment. As we have already noted, what primarily guarantees the planetary set is the bust of Saturn alone. Sol and Luna are the regular pair found in the upper corners of most tauroctonies. The fact that they are more than that, that in this relief they are also the first and last terms of a planetary sequence, depends (since we must initially exclude the other four) on the identification of the bust next to Sol as Saturn's. Since that bust lacks iconographic attributes and is merely that of an elderly male, bearded and with a full head of hair, that identification is not automatic. It rests, rather, on the following two considerations. First, by elimination, it is difficult to find any other identity. In that setting a wind god or a season would be conceivable, but it does not appear to be either of those. No other candidate comes to mind. Secondly, its pose in near profile is identical with the poses of Sol and Luna, indicating that the three belong in the same set. If that is so, then it can only be a planet; if a planet, then Saturn, and the rest follows. One further factor is relevant — the pose of Luna. Normally, when the faces of the luminaries are in profile, there is an asymmetry: while Sol is turned inwards to the scene enacted below, Luna looks outwards and away as if in sorrow or dissociation from the killing of her creature the bull. Here in the Bologna relief, unusually, both luminaries face inwards and the two busts are balanced. Clearly, there is an overriding purpose, and when

---

[247] *Mithras* (above, n. 4), 320.

we observe the pose of the presumed Saturn we see that the intention was to provide a balanced set of planetary gods in which the outer three on each side face inwards in profile leaving the central one, Jupiter, in full face.[248] We therefore conclude that, if indeed the upper central fragment is a restoration, its reconstruction is certain and that the busts of the planets stood in the original as they stand now. Consequently, the main arguments of the present study, which depend simply on the fact that there is — and always was — across the top of the Bologna relief a row of the seven deities in the week-day order from the Moon on the right to the Sun on the left, are unaffected.

[248] See above, pp. 30 ff. with n. 60.

INDICES

I. MONUMENTS

A. MITHRAIC MONUMENTS

1. *CIMRM*

B. Monuments of the cult of Jupiter Heliopolitanus:
Y. Hajjar, *La triade d'Héliopolis-Baalbek*

II. ANCIENT AUTHORS

III. GENERAL

LIST OF PLATES

PLATE I

PLATE II

PLATE III

PLATE IV

PLATE V

PLATE VI

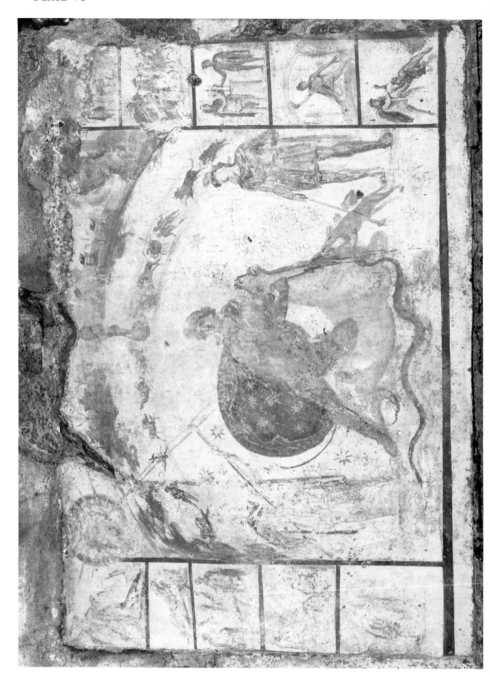

DATE DUE
